Praise

"I believe that everyone has a unique talent or skill and the trick in life is to match your talent to a market opportunity if you want to succeed in business. Mike's book, *The Entrepreneur's Roadmap*, can help you leverage your skill and with AI build a business to become the entrepreneur of your life."
— **Vernon W. Hill II**, Founder and Chairman Metro Bank; Former Founder, Chairman and CEO Commerce Bank (TD Bank US)

"Great plans rarely fail from lack of ambition; they falter in the long, often uncomfortable distance between inception and maturity – most commonly because of poor prioritization, the hidden adversary even of the most capable founder. In this essay Mike offers disciplined guidance that steadies and, when necessary, challenges founder instincts. He maps a clear route from early vision to lucrative exit. For any entrepreneur stuck despite good ideas and sustained effort, this is the roadmap to follow."
— **John Casey**, Co-Founder Noetic and Former President, CNBC International

"Mike brings a wealth of experience as a successful technology entrepreneur, investor, and mentor to his new book, *The Entrepreneur's Roadmap*. The book takes all his experience and knowledge and encapsulates it into an easy-to-read playbook for entrepreneurs to help them build a successful technology business. The speed of AI innovation, the cross current it is creating and the opportunities that are emerging, make this a must read for anyone that wants to build a successful business platform in this new AI world."

— **Walter "Buck" Buckley**, Founder and Managing Partner SemCap; Former Founder and CEO, Internet Capital Group (ICG)

"The Entrepreneur's Roadmap is a must-read for anyone with the ambition to create something truly impactful in a world of accelerating technological complexity and opportunity. Mike is a brilliant investor and serial entrepreneur, and this book provides the wisdom, clarity, and encouragement every founder needs on their journey."

— **Connor McMahan**, Founder and Managing Partner Virent Capital

"For anyone who ever had a dream of creating their own business, Michael has written *The Entrepreneur's Roadmap*. It gives a step-by-step framework that provides the resources, network and services to start, manage and exit a successful business. This Roadmap is your on-line assistant (coach) to help you utilize this ever-changing technology, called AI."

— **John T. Fries**, Co-Founder Neighborhood Health Partnership (United Healthcare)

"Major new platforms – AI being the biggest of our lifetime – open the field for entrepreneurs. True enough, AI will shift (or destroy) trillions in investor value. But, count on AI to create many trillions more, most by entrepreneurs who leverage its powers and build fast. Michael Carter's new book shows the way. Like a trusted mentor, *The Entrepreneur's Roadmap* will help you plan smartly, more decisively and adapt wisely. With millions of global entrepreneurs competing for AI's vast new riches. *The Entrepreneur's Roadmap* is your inside edge."

— **Rich Karlgaard**, Founder of *Upside Magazine*, Best-selling author, and legendary publisher of *Forbes*

"Mike is a successful author and experienced entrepreneur who has the ability to see around corners! This latest work of his highlights how to be one step ahead in this soon to be AI world."

— **Ira Lubert,** Founder of Independence Capital Partners

"Kudos to Mike Carter for providing the AI Entrepreneur (whom Mike characterizes as the athlete of the 21st century) with the ABC's of building their business. Mike recognizes that artificial intelligence is becoming an essential component of a myriad of known and to be known businesses. With that knowledge, and his decades of experience, he provides a very comprehensive playbook to take businesses from dream, through build, scale and, with skill and luck, a profitable exit."

— **Lisa Kapnick**, Chairman of *The Philadelphia Inquirer*

"Written by a proven and seasoned entrepreneur and accomplished author who sees the future, this book offers practical insights and real-world lessons to help founders turn their dreams and ideas into reality. Michael provides an empowering playbook on how to thrive in an AI democratized world."
— **Admiral Thomas C. Lynch**, Chairman New Day USA

"The prophet Zechariah wrote, 'not might, nor by power, but by my spirit, says the Lord of Hosts.' Mike's spirit, his integrity, ingenuity, and drive to succeed is revealed in *The Entrepreneur's Roadmap*. I encourage all new entrepreneurs to read this important book and keep on your desk for reference to what is required as a reminder of the grit, spirit, and know how required for today's entrepreneurs with AI."
— **Jerry Johnson**, Chairman and CEO Axum Advisors

"First and foremost, Mike is an amazing person and gifted serial entrepreneur. He is a proven and incredibly forward-thinking successful entrepreneur who focuses on cutting edge solutions. *The Entrepreneur's Roadmap* (EMG.AI) is a must have, easy to use solution for any entrepreneur at any level or stage in the business and pursuit of their dream. It greatly simplifies the business launch process, increases the likelihood of success, fuels powerful

growth through sound time-proven strategies and ultimately results in significantly higher exits."
— **Joe Giorno**, Founder of Ascending Angel Investments, LLC

"As a former founder and public-company CEO now serving on public and private boards, I look for one thing in startup playbooks: whether they turn energy into governance-grade execution. *The Entrepreneur's Roadmap* does. Michael's 73 deliverables, IP-first discipline, 'always-on' capital strategy, and scoreboarding mindset transform founder hustle into a cadence investors and boards can trust—one that readies a company not just to launch, but to scale, withstand scrutiny, and create lasting enterprise value in the AI era. For the founder who wants to build something enduring, this book is both compass and catalyst."
— **Tom Petro**, Author and Former CEO Fox Chase Bank

"We were blessed to find Mike and EMG while working with him and creating our AI Code Intelligence Company, The Code Registry. The Code Registry's mission is to democratize code knowledge in the age of AI. His roadmap is a proven way to create and grow your company, and has helped create, grow, and accelerate our company to be the fastest growing in our market."
— **Stephen Gray**, Co-Founder and CEO The Code Registry

"Written by a serial entrepreneur for entrepreneurs, *The Entrepreneur's Roadmap* celebrates and empowers today's star business athletes – entrepreneurs."
— **John Loftus**, Partner SemCap, former Managing Director Internet Capital Group

"Mike Carter and EMG has been a game-changer for my brother and my business, Highlander.AI. Mike has helped show us a path to create and grow our business. His book, *The Entrepreneur's Roadmap*, will help any entrepreneur looking to create and grow their business in the age of AI win."
— **Chandler Kline**, Co-Founder and CEO Highlander.AI

THE ENTREPRENEUR'S ROADMAP

Your guide to creating a winning business in the age of AI

MICHAEL MARSH CARTER

FOREWORD BY DANIEL PRIESTLEY

R^ethink

First published in Great Britain in 2026
by Rethink Press (www.rethinkpress.com)

© Copyright Michael Marsh Carter

All rights reserved. No part of this publication may be reproduced, stored in or introduced into a retrieval system, or transmitted, in any form, or by any means (electronic, mechanical, photocopying, recording or otherwise) without the prior written permission of the publisher.

The right of Michael Marsh Carter to be identified as the author of this work has been asserted by him in accordance with the Copyright, Designs and Patents Act 1988.

This book is sold subject to the condition that it shall not, by way of trade or otherwise, be lent, resold, hired out, or otherwise circulated without the publisher's prior consent in any form of binding or cover other than that in which it is published and without a similar condition including this condition being imposed on the subsequent purchaser.

Dedicated to my children, Harrison and Catherine, to help them on their own wonderful and mission-led entrepreneurial journeys in life; to my mentor, the legendary Warren V "Pete" Musser; and to Miles Frost, my guardian angel on my last journey. I hope that with EMG.AI, my new company, and this book, The Entrepreneur's Roadmap, *that we can be the agent for entrepreneurs around the world, helping to usher in the entrepreneur revolution.*

Contents

Foreword	1
Introduction	5
Why I'm writing this book	6
About me	11
The Mission Corporation	13
1 Entrepreneurs Are The Athletes Of The Twenty-First Century	**15**
Democratizing entrepreneurship	18
EMG: The agent for entrepreneurs	20
Entrepreneurs think differently	24
What is the Entrepreneur's Roadmap?	26
The seventy-three steps	29
What is a mission-driven entrepreneur?	32
A roadmap for entrepreneurs at any stage	35

2	**Company Creation**	**37**
	Company formation	38
	Liquid capital mapping	43
	Business (mission) model canvas	44
	Naming convention, branding, and design	46
	Choose professional advisers	47
	Creating legal documents and contracts	48
	Capitalization table creation and monitoring	50
	How the VC business will change with AI	54
	Intellectual property	58
	Thomas Edison and the power of invention	63
3	**Executing Your Company's Mission Through Action**	**65**
	Structuring your company for success	65
	Human capital mapping	67
	Roles and responsibilities	72
	Board formation	74
	Planning and formatting	77
	Product roadmapping	83
	3-2-1 mission activation	87

4	**Positioning Your Business For Success**	**91**
	How to build your mission deck	92
	Sales expansion, recruiting, and strategy	94
	Recruiting salespeople	98
	Brand voice/advertising	99
	Business process functional mapping	100
	Distinctive competency mapping	105
	Strategic partnering	106
	Recruiting talent	108
5	**Scoreboarding Your Business**	**113**
	Assets explained	113
	Capital raising	119
	New product development	124
	Protecting your invention: Registering IP	130
	Scoreboarding	133
6	**Planning Your Successful Exit**	**137**
	What's your business worth?	138
	Wealth and retirement planning	141
	Exit planning	144
	Selling your business	148
	Build your data room	150
	Exit mapping	151
	Exit your business successfully	154

7	**The New Age Of Entrepreneurship**	**159**
	The democratization of AI	160
	The role of the developer as cocreator developers	164
	Democratizing the VC industry	167
	Taxes: No longer a political issue	170

Conclusion: What Does The Future Look Like For Entrepreneurs?	**181**
Key takeaways from this book	185
What's next?	187

Acknowledgments	**189**
The Author	**191**

Foreword

We're living through an entrepreneurial revolution. Millions are walking away from traditional corporate jobs in search of more freedom, flexibility, fun—and yes, financial upside too.

For almost a century, there was no real alternative to climbing the corporate ladder. If you wanted access to the power and opportunity of the modern economy, you had to plug into a big brand or miss out entirely. That era is now over.

Today, the entrepreneurial spirit is not only alive, it's thriving. The most powerful media channels are owned by YouTubers. Megyn Kelly and Tucker Carlson reach more people broadcasting solo than they ever did within legacy news networks. The most successful bankers aren't climbing the ranks at Goldman Sachs, they're building their own funds, like Bill Ackman and Michael Burry, using their personal brands to attract capital and strike billion-dollar deals.

Since the early 2000s, social media, cloud computing, and mobile technology have given small businesses superpowers: media reach, e-commerce capabilities, and global, decentralized teams. Now, with the rise of artificial intelligence (AI), those superpowers are multiplying. Small teams can access capabilities once reserved for Fortune 500 companies—legal analysis, world-class marketing strategy, financial forecasting, graphic design, and data science—on demand, and nearly free.

This levels the playing field of opportunity. The barriers to entry have come crashing down and people from all walks of life are excited to create something themselves or to join a small dynamic team of rebels and misfits, instead of crawling into an office cubicle each day.

I have first-hand experience. In 2020, as the world was going into lockdown, my Co-Founder and I were launching a new business, ScoreApp.com. We had to do things differently. Everyone worked remotely, we built the brand on social media, pitched angel investors on Zoom calls and built our culture on Slack channels. Despite—or more likely because of—this new decentralized approach, we scaled up and were recognized as one of the fastest-growing tech companies in the UK. Today, the business continues to scale; it's highly profitable and valuable.

Make no mistake, entrepreneurship is not easy. For every approach that works, there are hundreds that fail. It's like aerodynamics: only a handful of designs fly; most crash on the runway.

What entrepreneurs need is a reliable flight plan—something grounded in data, shaped by real-world experience, and battle-tested by the best. That's exactly what Mike Carter offers in this book.

Mike has seen both sides. As a venture capitalist (VC), he reviewed thousands of pitches, backed founders with real potential, and coached them to win. Then he built BizEquity—a company that not only scaled successfully but also gave him access to one of the largest datasets in the world on private company valuations. He's helped tens of thousands of entrepreneurs understand what their business is really worth and what makes the difference between value creation and wasted effort.

I have enjoyed many conversations with Mike over the years that have led to inspirational insights. I've always encouraged him to share his wisdom with more people. Now he's here to help you.

This book is a roadmap. A set of principles. A distilled playbook for building a business that works—one that scales, stands out, and leaves a mark.

Read it. Use it. Go make your dent in the universe.

Daniel Priestley
Author of *Entrepreneur Revolution*,
Founder of Dent and ScoreApp

Introduction

It is my firm belief that the entrepreneur is the athlete of the twenty-first century and that AI will democratize entrepreneurship globally, making entrepreneurs the stars of tomorrow. Just as, two hundred years ago, the Industrial Revolution made mainstream the concept of having a "job," whereby you were paid by a business for dedicated service, AI will ignite the entrepreneurial revolution for millions, creating a new company—You. Your job will be "you," or the company that you can now create more easily and effectively.

Every person is the entrepreneur of their own life, and like my friend Rich Karlgaard says, "has their own hero's journey." The entrepreneur is the world's new hero, the person who defies all the odds, who lays everything on the line to accomplish things that most people can only dream of. As Steve Jobs, the founder of Apple, said toward the end of his chronicled life in his Stanford University's commencement speech, "Your time is limited, so don't waste it living someone else's life. Don't be trapped by dogma—which is living with the results of other people's thinking [...] have the courage to follow your heart and intuition."[1]

Today, we are in a new renaissance period when AI will make entrepreneurship accessible to everyone with a big dream and strong purpose. Anyone who wants to follow their inner voice and start a business of their own will be able to do so. It becomes more important than ever to remember these words and inspire your future. There has never been a better time to begin your own entrepreneurship journey.

Why I'm writing this book

This book is part of my mission to spread the good news that AI can and will be a force of good in people's lives. If harnessed correctly, it will unleash a new revolution: the "entrepreneur revolution" (as Daniel Priestley laid out so brilliantly in his best-selling book of the same name).[2] Daniel's book was published

---

1 Stanford, "Steve Jobs' 2005 Stanford Commencement Address" (8 March 2008), www.youtube.com/watch?v=UF8uR6Z6KLc, accessed 3 July 2025
2 D Priestley, *Entrepreneur Revolution: How to develop your entrepreneurial mindset and start a business that works* (Capstone, 2024)

before the AI revolution, which shows his foresight. With AI, entrepreneurship will be a much easier journey, and available to all. The greatest potential of AI lies in its ability to create more entrepreneurs. These new entrepreneurs will grow the economy and solve problems while creating solutions for humankind.

As redundant process-laden tasks and roles become commoditized in an instant, there is of course a risk that AI will displace millions of workers, but I think that shortchanges the God-given human potential we all have for creating the future and being the entrepreneurs of our own lives. AI has the real potential to change people's lives if harnessed properly by creating new types of work, and new industries. Individuals with agency will have a distinct advantage in this new world by leveraging the knowledge and capabilities that AI will make available to create new businesses in an instant. When there are millions more entrepreneurs, the workplace will change, and if skills are harnessed correctly, everyone will thrive.

The book you're holding now will become your journey's guide in the Age of AI to starting your business. It will teach you how to create, grow, and exit your business by helping you discover the essential steps you need to employ to help begin and execute your entrepreneurial dreams.

In my last book, *The Mission Corporation*, I laid out the idea that capitalism is the greatest economic system the world has ever known but that it could be better by being more purpose-driven and incentivized by governments around the world through having policies that support business creation and promote a healthy version of capitalism.[3] I premised that for capitalism to succeed in the next century, every business should have a purpose that is greater than itself. This thesis then became empirically proven through Ranjay Gulati's best-selling book on the most successful growth companies of the last twenty years, *Deep Purpose*.[4]

In this new book, I seek to provide a step-by-step guide on your journey as an entrepreneur to create these AI-enabled businesses of tomorrow. Business is the greatest vehicle of change in the world, and we need more and better entrepreneurs to usher in the new age of enlightenment and prosperity for all.

My goal with this book—and with my new company Entrepreneurs Management Group (EMG) Worldwide, Inc. and its application at EMG.AI—is to demystify entrepreneurship. I want to help to democratize it by putting every ounce of knowledge I have learned in building and investing in hundreds of technology-enabled businesses and learnings from my mentor, the legendary venture investor Warren V

---

3   MT Moe and MM Carter, *The Mission Corporation: How contemporary capitalism can change the world one business at a time* (Rethink Press, 2021)
4   R Gulati, *Deep Purpose: The heart and soul of high-performance companies* (Harper Business, 2022)

INTRODUCTION

"Pete" Musser, in one operating system, one platform, and one firm.

Warren V "Pete" Musser may well be the founder of VC for the East Coast of America. Pete created his firm, Safeguard Scientifics, to help entrepreneurs who were building technology-related businesses. He accomplished this over fifty years and three technological life cycles spanning mainframe computers, mini computing, and the internet revolution. Pete enabled thousands of entrepreneurs to achieve their goals and helped to create hundreds of thousands of jobs.

By supporting great entrepreneurs, Pete gave birth to many multi-billion-dollar industries. More importantly, he helped to mentor some of the best American entrepreneurs of the twenty-first century. Companies like Comcast, Novell, and QVC have Pete's fingerprints on their creation. Entrepreneurs like Ralph J Roberts, Joseph Segal, Walter Buckley, Ira M Lubert, and Frank and Michael Sanchez got their starts and inspiration from Pete. He also inspired and supported leaders like Admiral Thomas Lynch, Jerry Johnson, James K Sims, and even Eric Schmidt, whose first CEO job came through Pete. Most importantly, Pete continues to help thousands of people both in their careers and through the charities he gave to. He created an ethos rooted in humility and kindness, which many of us wish to continue sharing and passing on.

I was so blessed to work and learn from Pete and to be able to call him my friend and mentor. This book is a testament to him—a man who provided guidance on many of these entrepreneurial roadmap steps that we are now able to digitize and power through AI. Our team's commitment at EMG.AI is to help entrepreneurs to create companies with powerful missions that will change the world. Having a mentor as an entrepreneur has changed my life and enabled me to fulfill my own entrepreneurial dreams. It is our hope at EMG.AI that by creating the world's first-ever entrepreneurs' agent, we can act as a digital mentor to help millions of entrepreneurs to one day change theirs.

The mission at my last company, BizEquity, was to democratize business valuation knowledge, and we did that by creating the world's largest online platform to value a business. BizEquity has been used by over 400,000 businesses, and utilized by over 3,000 financial services firms and advisors. I successfully sold BizEquity in 2019 to a world-class entrepreneur and leader, Whitney Shaw, the CEO of his company ACBJ, the largest publisher of daily business information and news in over forty-five markets in the US, and a strategic business unit of Advance Media, the major investor and owner behind Reddit. Whit showed me how to lead through integrity, enabling team members' growth by meeting them where they are and leveraging their strengths. I am now on to my next entrepreneur journey with my new company,

EMG.AI, with an even bigger mission and purpose at this important time with the dawn of AI.

About me

I have been blessed in my life. I had loving parents, a devoted single mother who raised me, three older brothers that helped show me the right path, and a strong faith.

As a child I loved sports (racket sports particularly), but once I realized I would never be Björn Borg II or play at Wimbledon, I moved on. I became enamored by business and the role of entrepreneurs through *Forbes* magazine as a teenager. In this, my business bible, I read numerous inspirational stories about great entrepreneurs like Craig McCaw, Jeff Bezos, Phil Knight, Richard Branson, and Elon Musk and learned about the challenges that these successful entrepreneurs and business pioneers had faced. Instead of collecting baseball and football cards after the age of fourteen, I collected the stories of entrepreneurs.

I am now married, with a beautiful wife and two amazing children, Harrison and Catherine, who mean everything to me. I have started seven software companies, was an executive officer of one of the first publicly traded internet companies, and worked alongside the legendary venture investor Warren V "Pete" Musser, who became a mentor and a second father-like figure to me. Without Pete in my professional career and as a role model to pattern myself by, I would not have had much success. I was lucky.

Like all of you, life has had its challenges and has been a winding road, difficult at times. As a child, I had a debilitating speech problem, whereby I spoke as if I was deaf until the age of about eight. If it wasn't for my devoted mother and daily speech pathology lessons, my life would have been different. I also suffered with dyslexia and found school difficult. I had and still do have a very short attention span and suffer from what is now popularly called ADHD.

I consider these traits true blessings. I was able to see things differently from a young age and was forced to feel a bit different and not be afraid to go it alone at times. I had to make fast decisions based on information I could glean quickly and see patterns that others could not. I was forced to go with my gut, my intuition. These traits allowed me to develop stronger ones that I would rely on in my entrepreneurial career and nurture deep and lifelong relationships built upon trust and authenticity. I have only read a few books in my life from cover to cover, but I was able to author two—one of which was a best-selling book on entrepreneur-led economics and capitalism—and this will be my third and most important one.

Empathy is a God-given gift that you only gain insight into when life deals you minor (in my case) or major obstacles. These give you the ability to feel what others might be going through because you have felt something similar in your own journey, and so you can now relate to other people's challenges. One of the angels—or heroes—in my life whom I was blessed to meet, work with, and call a true friend, the late Miles Frost, would say his father, the legendary interviewer Sir David Frost, taught him that you can learn from everyone you meet. This is true because everyone has had their own journey made up of unique experiences and learnings. You never know what anyone has gone through, but you can always learn from their challenges because through adversity you learn great truths.

The Mission Corporation

In 2021 I published a book that I wrote during COVID called *The Mission Corporation* with my good friend and former board member at BizEquity, Mike Moe. This was a book about how business can change the world. Within the pages we discussed how capitalism, the greatest economic system the world had ever known, could get even better. The book was inspired by my journey with BizEquity and what I had seen in the capital markets and financing of start-ups. I noticed that entrepreneurs had come to be viewed as mere vessels by the investor class as private equity philosophies subsumed venture philosophies (meaning the missions or purposes of business took a back seat to decision science-oriented investors who were solely focused on short-term gains at the expense of long-term enterprise values).

The book was based upon Adam Smith, the father of modern economic theory and creator of modern capitalism. Smith had quite literally written the book on capitalism, *The Wealth of Nations*,[5] but he had authored an early work that few had heard of called *The Theory of Moral Sentiments*, which had given the moral basis on his economic theory.[6] It was in this book that he laid out the pillars upon which economics and capitalism could then prosper. Unfortunately, it had seemed at the time that capitalism was hijacked by those that never read Smith's earlier work and subscribed to self-defined autotheism of profits based upon logic and self. True conservatism and capitalism when originally conceived by Smith was based on something far greater than self.

We had great success with that book as we looked to help set the new foundation (we called them declarations) for creating mission corporations. *Mission Corporation* values were those I learned from the great writings of Adam Smith and my time and experience with the late great Pete Musser and my friend Miles Frost.

---

5 A Smith, *The Wealth of Nations: An inquiry into the nature and causes of the wealth of nations* (CreateSpace, 2014)
6 A Smith, *The Theory of Moral Sentiments* (Penguin Classics, 2010)

ONE

Entrepreneurs Are The Athletes Of The Twenty-First Century

Today there are over 582 million entrepreneurs around the world.[7] They range from your local baker to the newest global AI software entrepreneur. By 2040, we believe there will be over two billion entrepreneurs as AI drives down the cost and complexity of helping anyone conceptualize and create a business. Social media has helped—just as *Forbes* did for the past hundred years—to share these stories of success. TV shows such as *Shark Tank* and *Dragons' Den* and platforms like TikTok and YouTube have proliferated the idea that business and influencers are cool and entrepreneurship is something to

---

[7] Entreprenote, "Half a billion and counting: The global potential of ideas," *Medium* (27 June 2025), https://medium.com/entreprenote/half-a-billion-entrepreneurs-and-counting-the-global-potential-of-ideas-cb1d5d0455cc, accessed 18 August 2025

be admired and aspired to. Millions of young men and women finishing higher education in the next ten years will choose to pursue their dreams based on what they have seen. Entrepreneurship enabled by AI will be an aspiration for many, not a job at a Forbes' Global 2000 organization thousands of miles away from home.

Can you imagine what Steve Jobs would think of AI and its promise of liquid knowledge, relationships, networks, and capital? He would see it, as I do, as the fuel to enable every living person to be an entrepreneur and live their dreams.

In the eighteenth century, statesmen and military leaders like George Washington or Alexander Hamilton were the heroes. In the nineteenth century it was industrialists like Carnegie, Mellon, and Morgan. In the twentieth century, with the dawn of early movies and television, it was actors and actresses. In the late twentieth century and early millennium, it was athletes like Michael Jordan, Tiger Woods, and Tom Brady. Today, and for the next century or two, the entrepreneur will be the hero.

Unlike athletics, where natural-born phenoms can be sussed out early in a ten year old through organized sports, where they're then put on the fast track to top tier college athletics, becoming pros after years of coaching and academies, entrepreneurs are both born and made. Some of the greatest entrepreneurs became so by chance. For Phil Knight, the founder of Nike and of *Shoe Dog* fame, it was his personal journey and life experience that made him an entrepreneur.

Other entrepreneurs, like me, are those who have always felt different, who have gone through something in their lives at a young age where they needed to prove something to themselves and others to find meaning in their own success. Most want to be entrepreneurs and bosses of their own lives, but they just haven't taken their shot at their dream because they never had a mentor or a knowledge base to support them to do so. Harvard is not an entrepreneur factory, thank goodness. Life is.

Historically, less than 1% of those born will pursue their entrepreneurial dreams during their lifetime. Worse, 99.99992% of all start-ups will *never* receive the investment support, VC, or private equity capital to fuel their businesses. 90% of all businesses started will fail to survive after five years.

Clearly, the deck is stacked against these early entrepreneurs. Why? It's not just about having the capital to fulfill their product build-outs and hire the employees and team members they need to achieve their entrepreneurial ambitions. It's much more than that. It's because of the lack of the whole stack of things you need as an entrepreneur to succeed. You need knowledge of the things you need to do; the connections and network of people and professionals to help you. You need not just the capital but a mentor to help guide you and believe in you when the chips are down on your journey, because inevitably they will be.

Democratizing entrepreneurship

What if that stack of things entrepreneurs needed to do—the actual deliverables—could be democratized with the help of AI? What if you could have at your fingertips all the essential executables you need to get done at every step of your entrepreneurial journey and a network of resources to assist you? What if you could have your own digital mentor to support you and keep you in line if you get off track? Tomorrow, that will not just be a great vision of the future but the reality of AI. AI will be the democratizing force to usher in a new era of entrepreneurship for the world. It's an exciting time.

Today, if you ask high school students around the world what they want to do with their lives, a staggering 75% of them want to become entrepreneurs.[8] Historically, those dreams fade quickly as they become professional students. They get into universities, take on student debts, and study things that were constructed by the education complex of fifty years

---

8   V Zainzinger, "75% of students want to start a business," *Real Business* (14 September 2012), https://realbusiness.co.uk/75-of-students-want-to-start-a-business, accessed 18 August 2025

ago. They trade their dreams for finding a job with someone else so they can pay off their student loans and debts. They leave their communities, their families, and their mates and settle for lives that aren't necessarily their hero's journey.

Mark Twain once said, "The most important days in your life are the day you were born, and when you find out the reason why"—when you discover your purpose or mission. As my friend and the legendary publisher of *Forbes*, Rich Karlgaard, said to me in conversation, "Everyone has a hero's journey and everyone is the entrepreneur of their own lives."

AI has the chance to democratize entrepreneurship by helping to make it not just more affordable than ever to build out the entrepreneur's dreams but more available too. Like the industrial revolution made muscle power liquid, AI will make brain power and the critical knowledge, capital, relationships, and resources more liquid. Today, every entrepreneur will have the collective wisdom of the smartest people in the world available if they know where to look and how to ask and frame their questions or prompts.

> **CASE STUDY: The IMG story**
>
> In 1960 an attorney from Cleveland Ohio met Arnold Palmer—a young, dynamic, tremendously talented, and charismatic golfer—and created a new type of firm that was dedicated to the athlete. The mission

> was to help the athlete by becoming their trusted adviser, advocate, agent, and a one-stop shop for all things related to their profession and craft. That man, Mark McCormack, created IMG (now called IMG Endeavor), the most important company ever made to help create successful athletic careers. IMG was created to be the trusted adviser, the one hand the athlete would shake that would handle all aspects of their business affairs. Mark knew that athletes didn't know all the aspects of businesses that they needed to know, and he created a professional services firm to support them.
>
> Today, IMG is a multi-billion-dollar media business that creates, produces, and licenses businesses for over 10,000 athletes and Hollywood stars across the globe. It has academies that train them, production studios that produce shows, and a plethora of supporting services and companies to help support them.

EMG: The agent for entrepreneurs

It's time for a new type of firm to be created, one that is dedicated to the entrepreneur. Like athletes and the Hollywood/Bollywood stars before them, the entrepreneur needs an agent and an agency to help support them as they grow. A person or firm that can be the go-to resource for all their needs while they pursue their missions. A firm that can provide the resources, connectivity, and capital to fuel their dreams and prepare them for tomorrow. With the dawn of AI, this agent can and will be digital. The agent needs to be a mentor to help the entrepreneur to succeed and grow, and the agency a company purpose-built to support them.

Today, entrepreneurs and business owners have to deal with:

- Attorneys
- Government and state regulations
- Domain registries
- Executive coaches
- Website developers
- Software programmers
- Technology (hosting, infrastructure, and security) providers
- AI experts
- Marketing and branding consultants
- Digital marketing agencies
- Social media consultants
- Intellectual property (IP) registries
- Logo creators
- Private and angel investors
- Accountants

- Public relation firms
- Investor relation firms
- Real estate providers
- Payroll providers
- VC firms
- IP experts
- Management consultants
- Human capital and talent consultants
- Insurance providers (liability, directors' and officers' (D&O), health, and life)
- Tax consultants
- Wealth managers
- Exit planners
- Mergers and acquisitions (M&A) advisers

The success of entrepreneurs globally is dependent not only on their talents, commitment, and skill but also the resources, network, and services they can draw upon to help them achieve success.

Technology-enabled businesses

Every business today is in some way a software company. All businesses now have software assets to run their websites and mobile apps, and power their sales, marketing, and financial systems. Mark Andreessen, the founder of one of the top VC firms in the world today, Andreessen Horowitz, stated, "Software is eating the world."[9] This is true, but if software is indeed "eating the world," then AI is clearly its teeth. Every business today is a software company because every business has a website, a mobile app, a social media presence, a portal, a payments system they integrate to, a customer relationship management (CRM) system to track prospects and clients, and an accounting system to manage the books.

In the next five years, every one of these software systems will change and evolve to help businesses run their operations more efficiently. The systems and sites will be utilizing AI to make them smarter and more intuitive. Businesses will become entities with a brain. That brain will take the form of an AI agent—going beyond just a business intelligence software tool, it will be truly core to the business. Our focus at EMG is to work with entrepreneurs as they build and scale their businesses, which will become or already are software or digital businesses. Technology-enabled or digital businesses are based upon software. Software is the fabric upon which all businesses exist and operate, and in the future AI will be the fuel to power them.

---

9   M Andreessen, "Why software is eating the world," *Andreessen Horowitz* (20 August 2011), https://a16z.com/why-software-is-eating-the-world, accessed 4 July 2025

Entrepreneurs think differently

It is said that entrepreneurs are like stars, born not made. We are all born to be the entrepreneur of our own lives. Most people, however, never pursue their own dreams and missions to seek life's purpose. The reason for this has to do with not having the right mentors to help show them the path and also because most people don't have the resources of capital or knowledge to pursue their dreams. Whether you are a care provider or nurse, a teacher, a doctor, an attorney, a machinist, or an engineer, you all will have the chance in the future to create your own businesses, even if you work for others.

True entrepreneurs that have already started their businesses—or are dreaming of building them—are already there. Entrepreneurs think differently; they see things others don't or can't see yet, much like an athlete may have a unique skill that differentiates them on how to dribble, shoot, kick, swing, serve, drive, or throw. Entrepreneurs in any given space or market do things differently. Intuition and agency are crucial for this new generation of entrepreneurs to harness the power of AI applications and the knowledge all around them.

Entrepreneurs have special talents

Entrepreneurs come from every walk of life. Their lives shape their skills. Their talents can range from selling the invisible, marketing feelings, cultivating talent, and creating content to technology engineering, business operations, relationship building, ecosystem development, or even simple problem solving. Entrepreneurs' talents are not made in school; they are made through and by life. They usually think outside the box and dream of doing things differently in any given market, and they attract cadres of people to them. Entrepreneurs can operationalize missions and mobilize talent.

Athletes have coaches

No matter how great they are, every athlete who plays a sport—whether at amateur or professional level—has or has had a coach that helps them to achieve their potential. That coach helps them achieve their goals and pushes them to new heights. That coach grades them at every step to help them get better. That coach helps to advise them on what they can be doing great and what they can be doing even better. Guillermo Vilas had Tiriac, Andre Agassi had Bollettieri, Michael Jordan had Jackson, Messi had Rijkaard, and Carl Lewis had Tellez.

Entrepreneurs—as we have said, trademarked, and coined—are the athletes of the twenty-first century, yet nearly all of them have no coach. The lucky ones had a mentor that they learned from or shadowed. I was blessed to have Pete Musser so I know how having a good mentor can change the trajectory of your dreams, your entrepreneurial journey, and even your life. For the 0.2% of entrepreneurs that receive venture funding or angel investment,[10] that mentor can come from the investor, but only if that investor is world class and has done it before. What are we going to do for nearly all the entrepreneurs in the world in the next 100+ years who need help and a mentor?

One of the great promises of AI is in making knowledge liquid and helping to manufacture know-how. What we want to do at EMG.AI is not just provide the know-how but the know-*who*. Knowledge will be liquid as we will discuss through our Entrepreneur's Roadmap, but networks and connections of people to help coach will also be democratized and made liquid. Our mission is to help match entrepreneurs from around the world with agents or coaches in a sense that are AI enabled but also physical. Agents that can help them achieve their goals. That is the promise that AI can help make evident and we hope to share one day through our company.

What is the Entrepreneur's Roadmap?

When I was starting out, and then in my second job, I joined a team of fifty-five internet services professionals to rethink how internet consulting services could be reimagined in my role of chief marketing

---

10 D Stangler, I Tareque and A Morelix, "Annual Survey of Entrepreneurs Data Briefing Series," Ewing Marion Kauffman Foundation, www.kauffman.org/wp-content/uploads/2019/12/ASE-Briefing-1216_FINAL.pdf, accessed 18 August 2025

officer for US Interactive. I started with reimagining before subscription services were created, how clients could consume virtual products and services. I thought that instead of just billing for time and materials and pricing things by the hour, or even fixed time–fixed price consulting deliverables, what if for every project for a consulting client we could deliver an electronic or e-roadmap to show them how the internet would revolutionize their business? This became our main strategic thrust or differentiator. It enabled us to grow to 2,000-strong professionals and to go public and float our business on the NASDAQ. The e-roadmap was our go-to-market strategy and our reason for being.

Today, with EMG, we are creating a new type of roadmap for the entrepreneur: the Entrepreneur's Roadmap, which can provide to anyone starting, growing, or exiting a business the steps they need to take and the help they need to employ to make it to their own promised land. A roadmap to be used by drivers to get from point A to point B before Google Maps or Waze. The metaphor still applies for an entrepreneur. That is why we created and filed a patent on the world's first ever automated-through-AI strategic roadmap to help guide you as you build your business to move forward. You can't go where you need to go unless you know how to get there—the Entrepreneur's Roadmap will be your guide. Every entrepreneur will one day have an agent that can create them a personalized roadmap to success on their entrepreneurial journey.

What are the roadmap deliverables?

Nearly ten years ago, while traveling from London back to my home to Philadelphia for my last company on what was a tough day, I thought about what I had learned in building seven software companies and being part of some successful (and some not-so-successful) businesses and venture investments.

What would I do next if I was not doing or couldn't do what I was currently doing, but knowing what I knew now? I thought, wow, if only I could help every entrepreneur learn what I had learned after raising over US$200 million in VC money and helping to build businesses that served thousands of clients and employed hundreds of people. That would be what I would want to do next. If only I could codify that knowledge in a simple, powerful form and harness an enterprise to accomplish it. If I could do that, I thought, that would be my new mission and purpose in life besides being a good dad.

I thought of the best format that I ever created in conveying a marketing concept. Then I remembered the e-roadmap I created while I was the CMO of US Interactive, one of the first-ever publicly traded billion-dollar internet professional services firms.

What was it exactly I had to nail down for my businesses to move forward at every step? What had I learned in creating, growing, and exiting my businesses? I began listing over the course of the six-and-a-half-hour flight every step, deliverable, or thing I had to figure out along the journey. Some were obvious, others were not, and most took time to fully grasp and understand, which would only have come with trial and error and experience.

That journey and set of things that I listed down would be in the form of the infamous roadmap I created in 2000, but this time I would use the same visualization to provide guidance to the entrepreneur for every deliverable that he or she would need to do or be asked by their board or their investors to accomplish. These items wouldn't be esoteric leadership videos or hints but would actually be the down and dirty things I had to accomplish, the things I needed to put in place for the companies that had to be executed upon. That list, which a couple of years ago stood at 123 items, became the Entrepreneur's Roadmap, and would boil down to the seventy-three most essential deliverables.

The seventy-three steps

The Entrepreneur's Roadmap breaks down every deliverable that most entrepreneurs—especially those running technology-enabled businesses—will need to know. In creating the roadmap, that knowledge of the essential deliverables was codified around three core areas of focus or stages of the company:

1. The create phase
2. The growth phase
3. The exit phase

Each phase has a set of deliverables and tasks to execute to make your journey's destination readily available and more achievable.

The creation phase

The creation phase starts with the entrepreneur having the idea and beginning to lay out everything they need to do from the initial gestation phase. Everything from the legal setting up of a company, with the pros and cons of each legal structure, to creating your own company's logo and domain.

From there, we delve into the actual things you will need to do, from attracting capital into your business to hiring and bringing on contractors or employees. The roadmap serves not just as a guide in physical form, made available to all who go to our site at EMG. AI, but also provides online assistance, harnessing the power of AI to give you deep dive definitions at every step of the journey and facilitating introductions to resources that can assist you at every step.

The growth phase

The growth phase is focused on helping the entrepreneur move into the phase of attracting clients, keeping existing clients, and more advanced ways to measure and accelerate your business and its team. The growth phase sets in place those things that investors and boards will ask you to better measure your performance and achieve your pro forma goals. It ranges from helping you execute financially, to discover your business value and the levers to help you grow that value, all the way to building a performance culture inside your business to succeed.

The exit phase

The exit phase is focused on preparing your business for sale. As my friend Daniel Priestley likes to say:

> "You will exit your business one day; everyone will. You will either exit your business through a planned sale (hopefully), a death and estate sale, passing it on to team members through an ESOP program, or unfortunately shutting it down."

Our goal, using the exit phase and our roadmap, is to better prepare for a successful exit; to help you prepare before you get an offer or begin a process with an investment banker. Everything from exit plan mapping to finding the right wealth adviser to managing your proceeds is contained in our roadmap.

What is a mission-driven entrepreneur?

We are leaving an era of mercenary entrepreneurship, powered by venture capital, and entering a new era of missionary founders, powered by crowd-funding and angel investors. Missionary entrepreneurs would create their companies even if success through the selling or floating of their companies did not exist. They are mission-driven entrepreneurs, who are building their companies with a heart of a non-profit and the brains of a for-profit. Their purpose is their guide.

Mission-driven entrepreneurs have a purpose of being. They have created their companies because it is all they could think about creating. They have found a niche—or as the great Peter Thiel writes about in his seminal work, *Zero to One*—a market so big that others didn't dream it could be created.[11]

A great example of a mission-driven entrepreneur is the world's first trillionaire, Elon Musk. Yes, success through monetary accomplishment has followed Elon, but his purpose for building his empire has more meaning. Elon put it all on the line after PayPal took loans against his assets to build out Tesla and SpaceX. A more straightforward example of a mission-driven entrepreneur is the founder of Patagonia, who has used his company as a vessel for giving focused around environmental causes that supported their

---

11 P Thiel, *Zero to One: Notes on startups, or how to build the future* (Currency, 2014)

brand ethos. According to Patagonia, they have given 1% of their sales since 1985 to charity representing over US$230 million thus far.[12] Whether or not an entrepreneur gives back through their business, a mission-driven entrepreneur is driven by visions for the future. Their life's work becomes their mission through their businesses.

Goes beyond profit

Winston Churchill once said, "We make a living by what we get, but a life by what we give." The Jesuits teach that a life of service to others is what it's all about. You can achieve both goals and missions for your life through business. Business is the greatest force of change the world will ever know, if harnessed properly and with the right mission or purpose.

Profit is how businesses can be fueled to grow in the Age of AI. In the age of the internet, with the likes of Amazon that took nearly twenty years to reach profitability, investor capital was the fuel. Today, time to money or time to profit will be measured by more traditional means, profits; the reason being you no longer need US$10 million, hundreds of employees, and dozens of engineers to build your companies.

---

12 "1% for the Planet," Patagonia, https://eu.patagonia.com/gb/en/one-percent-for-the-planet.html, accessed 18 August 2025

You need the right idea at the right time, a powerful mission, and a roadmap to execute on your purpose, in order to succeed. In the next few years, there will be thousands of companies created for under US$200,000, with fewer than ten employees, which reach a market valuation and exit value of over US$100 million. In the next five years, we will discover the first billion-dollar company created with a team of five or fewer. Why? AI will be the democratizing force that entrepreneurship has needed. Beast mode will no longer be in a self-driving car like Tesla but in the form of company creation through AI, and hopefully one day through EMG.AI.

Profit will be the new deciding factor by which companies and entrepreneurs are judged. No longer will it be based upon the pitch or the school you attended to attract the right venture capitalists to bid your company's value higher. Business valuations like BizEquity.com will be the basis of the enterprise value you create through profit and revenue growth multiples. To truly build the company of tomorrow and to be a real mission-driven entrepreneur, it will be what you do with your profit in building your company that will make you a success—in life. Successful businesses that have the highest customer satisfaction, the lowest churn of clients, and the happiest, most fulfilled employees will be those that make their missions their purpose. Profit will just be the fuel in the tank to achieve that purpose and to ensure your successful exit.

A roadmap for entrepreneurs at any stage

The Entrepreneur's Roadmap was created to serve as an automated, AI-enabled guide online to help entrepreneurs at every stage of their journey create, grow, and exit their businesses. The steps that I learned, and thousands of other successful technology entrepreneurs have gone through, is now codified in one useful guide to help you plan for your future and succeed in your business. The roadmap will not just help you launch your business but will see it through to a successful exit for you and your stakeholders.

For too long the knowledge entrepreneurs needed to build their companies was hidden. The knowledge of the steps, the relationships, and the networks of talent to accomplish them were held by the few. Venture firms protected this knowledge as their proprietary networks. It never saw the light of day. Failures were kept private, and success was just a headline. By making the seventy-three steps that every entrepreneur needs freely available, it will help to unlock the key to success. Building a great company doesn't just start with a great idea or an enlightened mission; the mission needs a shepherd. EMG.AI and our patent-pending Entrepreneur's Roadmap seeks to be your guide in the Age of AI to assist you on your journey.

TWO
Company Creation

Your journey begins with your purpose, or mission, and your vision for what you want to create and build. The creation phase of your journey entails many steps to ensure you are properly on your way to achieving your dreams and goals with your business. Many of the things you have to get done in this phase may seem mundane or just milestones you have to check off to get things moving; many can simply be outsourced to the professional services firms you may already know. These are all important stops on your roadmap to success, and you can't skip them.

Legal issues or dealing with an attorney is often the first place many entrepreneurs start. That selection is ripe with decisions and challenges that you should be aware of. Forming and creating a company is so much more than that. You need to lay out all the essential steps and deliverables you need to have nailed down to begin developing, marketing, and selling your product or service to your desired market. Having the right framework or roadmap to begin the journey is key. Considering all the options and making the right decisions on each is essential.

This chapter seeks to help you by shining a light on the key deliverables or tasks you have to get done so you can successfully launch your company.

Company formation

What may seem like a mundane legal issue that can be simply outsourced to the nearest attorney—or the attorney you may know best or that someone introduces you to—is an important step in your journey. There are many ways you can form your entity. Each is steeped in their own complexity that will matter to you when you exit your business. Tax consequences, reporting complexity, and governance complexity and reporting should come first and foremost when you choose your company structure. It is often said to think always about the exit in mind. Nothing can be more important when you start than the legal entity stricture you create.

Forming a company in the United States and the United Kingdom involves several steps, including selecting a business structure, choosing a business name, registering the business, obtaining necessary licenses and permits, and opening a business bank account, all of which are intertwined and related. Different structures with the legal entity you form have different pros and cons, as we go into at EMG. AI. In the US, it was popular to form your entity as a limited liability company (LLC) due to the ability not to have double taxation; however, that entity type is now not as popular as it once was.

Other entity structures, such as a qualified C Corporation, now hold tax advantages if you qualify on exit to have a special one-time-reduced capital gains rate. Capital gains are the taxes a business or individual shareholder or entrepreneur would receive at an exit. Historically, for the last twenty years, that capital gains rate (before state taxes) was 20% and LLCs provided the best way to ensure that rate. With the rise of new policies and measures to promote entrepreneurship—as was seen in the UK with the Business Asset Disposal Relief and now a qualified C Corporation in the US—that rate can go down to as little as 10%.

Additionally, VC firms typically have not taken to LLC structures. If and should your company become "venture fundable," that legal structure would have changed to a C Corporation at the investor's discretion. I have also found, as an entrepreneur who has created companies in both forms (LLCs and C Corporations), that the extra reporting with LLCs, which is in the form of annual K-1s or tax financial stubs for individual shareholders, may be cumbersome. If you plan to build a tightly controlled or lifestyle business in the US with only one or two shareholders, LLC's with their single taxation structure is still an elegant solution.

The first table is a quick comparison of each structure (more can be seen on EMG.AI).

	LLC	C-Corp	S-Corp	Partnership	Sole Prop
Liability protection	Strong	Strong	Strong	Limited	None
Taxation	Pass-through	Double (21% + personal)	Pass-through	Pass-through	Personal rates
Formation cost	$50-500	$100-1,000+	$100-1,000+	$0-200	$0-50
Annual compliance	Moderate	High	High	Low	Minimal
Owner limits	Unlimited	Unlimited	100 max	2+	1
Capital access	Limited	Excellent	Limited	Moderate	Poor

This next table highlights some of the pros and cons of each structure.

	Overview	Advantages	Disadvantages	Best for
LLC	Most popular, combines liability protection with operational flexibility.	• Personal asset protection • Pass-through taxation • Flexible management structure • Fewer compliance requirements • Tax election options	• Self-employment taxes • Limited investor appeal • State-specific rules • Transfer regulations	Small-medium businesses seeking protection and flexibility.
C-Corp	Traditional corporate structure for businesses planning significant growth or seeking investment.	• Unlimited growth potential • Easy capital access • Perpetual existence • QSBS tax benefits • Multiple stock classes	• Double taxation • Complex regulations • High compliance costs • Formal management structure	High-growth start-ups seeking investment.

Cont.

Cont.

	Overview	Advantages	Disadvantages	Best for
S-Corp	Tax designation offering pass-through taxation with corporate liability protection.	• Avoids double taxation • Self-employment tax savings • Liability protection • Transferable ownership	• 100 shareholder limit • US citizen requirement • One stock class only • Strict compliance	Small businesses with fewer than 100 shareholders.
Partnership	Shared ownership for two or more people with simple formation but limited liability protection.	• Easy to establish • Combined expertise • Shared financial burden • Minimal regulations	• Unlimited liability • Shared debts • Potential conflicts • Limited life	Multiple owners collaborating.
Sole Prop	Simplest structure for individual owners with no legal separation from business.	• Full control • All profits to owner • Simple tax filing • Low start-up costs	• Unlimited liability • Personal asset risk • Limited capital access • Business ends with owner	Individual owners with minimal risk.

Liquid capital mapping

The ability to attract capital into your business for many technology-enabled or software-based businesses that rely on a capital investment to build out its product or service is key. What we like to do and believe is vital to success is to lay out in the early days a framework to judge and look for avenues to capital. These avenues or roads to capital can range from angel investing, friends and family capital rounds of finance, crowdfunding, and even VC, depending on your location or history of success. For first-time founders, it is vital to lay out all the alternatives in the early stages. Luckily for you, we are entering the age of crowdfunding when financing your company will get easier and more liquid. In the old days, finding friends, family, or angel investors was the only way to fuel your company.

The days of episodic fundraising are over. Gone are the days of waiting to raise money right before your existing round of capital is diminished. Fundraising, as it is popularly called, will now be evergreen, meaning it is an ongoing process. Every entrepreneur will be able to have an icon on their site, their app, or their social media presence that will seamlessly guide investors to their funding portal to receive capital because of new rules and capabilities of crowdfunding. Today, crowdfunding has become even more democratized with new legislation allowing companies to access millions of potential investors more easily.

In 2019, the US passed Regulation Crowdfunding (RegCF) legislation, which allowed anyone to invest up to 5% of their net worth in any/most private businesses. The Securities and Exchange Commission have to date authorized nearly 400 crowdfunding portals to help. At EMG we have a partnership with one of only thirty active RegCF and successful crowdfunding portals at Highlander.AI. Highlander does the work for you to help you market your company to prospective investors.

In fact, we believe in the promise of crowdfunding so much we are partnering with Highlander.AI to create FounderStudio.AI. This will be the first live and recorded streamed investment channel and network just for entrepreneurs to help them access capital from investors who can help their businesses grow.

Business (mission) model canvas

The business model canvas is a new technique and template that has emerged as a model to structure and lay out a business plan. The old way of constructing a business plan was based upon highly narrative and long-form writing, which could reach hundreds of pages in length. This new approach is powerful in its simplicity and focus on what truly matters for a business. While a traditional business plan is high on words, the business model canvas is high on visual representation.

Business Name: Designed By: Date: Version:

WHAT IS YOUR BUSINESS'S MISSION?	VALUE PROPOSITION	CUSTOMER SEGMENTS		AUDIENCE ENGAGEMENT
			REVENUE STREAMS	
	COSTS	CORE TASKS AND ASSETS		ENTREPRENEUR NOTES
KEY MARKETING FUNCTIONS				

Business (mission) model canvas

The rationale behind it is that businesses change and evolve, and founders should be focused on executing its product or services vision around key areas, including its customers, value proposition, infrastructure, and finances. The nine "building blocks" of the business model canvas was initially created in 2005 by Alexander Osterwalder, based on his PhD work supervised by Yves Pigneur on business model ontology.[13]

At EMG we believe that your mission or purpose should be at the center of your canvas and the primary driver for your business. You should take an iterative and active approach on updating your business model canvas with your team as you grow and evolve your business.

Naming convention, branding, and design

Branding is both an art and a science. Your brand is a feeling your customers, prospects, investors, and team members have when they think about your company and its mission and look at its name, logo, and web, social, or app presence. It is often overlooked, but it's possibly one of the most strategic and inexpensive things you can create as an entrepreneur, which will have the most lasting impact. AI has revolutionized

---

13 A Osterwalder (2004), "The Business Model Ontology—A proposition in a design science approach," PhD Thesis, University of Lausanne, Switzerland

branding too—sites like Design.com and services such as EMG.AI make it easier for you to get started.

Your sales and marketing imaging all flow from the brand or presence you create for your company. In the old days it was easy to discern who was well funded and used a high-end agency to design their materials and presence. Today, it is one-hundredth of the cost of the old days in the first internet revolution.

Design is an art form, and your design and branding parameters can help you attract the audience you need. Like everything on the entrepreneurial journey, it is all intertwined. Your goal should be to create a masterpiece organizationally. The most fun part is thinking about and creating with your outsourced providers what your name, brand, and design should represent.

Choose professional advisers

Professional advisers are services firms, or subject matter experts as contractors that specialize in areas that are not core to what you are doing as an entrepreneur or what your background has been. What I mean by that is that an entrepreneur should focus on what is core to their business and what they have unique expertise in to drive. Usually that is creating and building your product or service, finding and closing clients and strategic partners, and recruiting your team and advisory board members. Context would be those items like legal, accounting, tax planning, financial reporting, recruiting, technology development (sometimes), payroll, health insurance, wealth planning, and M&A advising. Each of these context services you need are critical decisions you have to make to ensure you are fielding the best team to accomplish your goals.

Finding the right professional advisers who will help you to grow your business and won't cost you an arm and a leg is crucial. You want them to work with you and to believe in your mission and vision for the company. Often, I have found that if they personally invested in you and your company, these advisers will go beyond the services they provide and will be important conduits to relationships that can grow your company, outside of the particular expertise they are providing you with. Together, all these firms make up an ecosystem, a close connected network of people and relationships that you can leverage to grow your business. EMG.AI was created to help you mitigate and discern professional advisers by serving as your digital and physical agent or mentor to bring the best talent and services to you and your company.

Creating legal documents and contracts

The legal aspects of company creation are something that all entrepreneurs need to quickly get in front of and nail down, even in the early days. The ability to work with an attorney and/or a law firm that is entrepreneurially focused is critical. All law firms and lawyers are not created equal. Law school teaches future attorneys to think critically and find what is off or wrong in every case they read or situation they are presented with. It is the rare attorney that seeks to understand not just the risk but the opportunity that separates those that are best at working with entrepreneurs. Over the last twenty-five years, I have seen great attorneys as well as high-priced ones that weren't particularly helpful to entrepreneurs.

I have always liked to use multiple attorneys and firms. You'll want one attorney to help with the formation documents that you will need. These include company formation, legal contracts with future clients (even if you don't have them yet), employee documents (NDAs and non-compete agreements), and employee stock option agreements, to name a few. I then use an IP specialist and an IP attorney to help draft patent and trademark agreements. I also like to use a global or larger firm for any large financing or M&A agreements.

It is vital you have the best legal representation you can have at every point. Cost is one of those things that, with proper diligence and referrals from EMG. AI, you can mitigate the capital risk versus the reward. Again, the concept of beginning with the end in mind is crucial. Entrepreneurs should have a bundle of documents in a data room, even during the initial creation phase of the business. Trust me, you will be happy that you do.

Capitalization table creation and monitoring

The capitalization (cap) table is the list of shareholders that make up the 100% equity in your business. Properly creating and maintaining a cap table will separate the wheat from the chaff—entrepreneurs that do this are on top of the most important but sometimes mundane details. Proper tracking and monitoring of your cap table shows your investors and strategic exit partners that they are dealing with an entrepreneur who is on top of things. Not capturing the cap table early or monitoring it properly leads to misunderstandings with investors or employees who may hold options as part of their total compensation.

Cap tables are important elements and board artifacts that will streamline funding rounds.

EXERCISE: Capitalization table

One of the core things to do as a founder of a business when adding team or board members who will receive equity, or you are beginning a fund or capital raising process, is to establish a capitalization table.

COMPANY CREATION

The five fundamental elements to this are:

1. The pre-money valuation of your business. This is the valuation of your business before new capital or investment is made. BizEquity.com is a good resource to use. Your pre-money valuation will be based on your IP and your pro forma financial projections.
2. The amount of capital you have raised or plan on raising to fund your business.
3. The post-money valuation of your business. This is your pre-money valuation plus the investment capital. For example, if your pre-money valuation is US$3,000,000 and you raise US$1,000,000, your post-money valuation is £4,000,000. In this case, the investor received 25% of the equity of the business for that US$1,000,000. The equity figure is always derived on the post-money valuation. Here, the dilution, or amount of equity that was decreased from the founding shareholders, is 25%.
4. The total number of shares of the business.
5. The number of shares and equity percentage of each shareholder.

The following is an example of a great online capitalization tool and service from Highlander.AI.

Financing is no longer episodic

Financing that is raising investment or debt capital to create your product or service or grow your business has historically been episodic, that is at a point of time. Often, that point of time occurred when you as

Example of an online capitalization tool, courtesy of Highlander

COMPANY CREATION

an entrepreneur or company have run out of money and have thirty, sixty, or ninety days before you could make payroll.

My mentor and hero Pete Musser had a great line he would say when meeting a company who presented their pro forma (future) financial projections when looking for capital or money. Pete would say that you want an entrepreneur that could dream and would be optimistic about the company's potential because without that there would be no hope or vision for the product or service. He would say, "Divide what the entrepreneur presents as to their revenue potential in half and see if it works and then divide the half in half again and see if the company lives." What that means is that when presenting their financing, an entrepreneur needs to show pro forma financials and their capital needs. It is important for entrepreneurs to realize this when they are presenting their financial projections and be sure that the capital requirements they need to support their headcount and development needs are properly represented.

Today, and in the future, capital raising for entrepreneurs and businesses will no longer need to be episodic; they will be constant or evergreen. All companies will have the opportunity to add an "invest now" button on their websites and app presences. Having your pitch deck and financials done in a professional manner and constantly updated will be key, as capital raising will be ongoing. Global crowdfunding, with the advent of AI, will allow this and ensure company financial and market transparency occurs. Services like Highlander.AI and FounderStudio.AI will be important vehicles to leverage for all entrepreneurs to grow. VC has been democratized. Everyone can be an investor today and every person can become an entrepreneur with the right help and guidance.

How the VC business will change with AI

AI has reduced the cost of starting a technology-enabled start-up business by 80% according to our own research at EMG.AI. Sam Landman, Co-Founder and general partner of a leading VC, Mosaic, says:

> "Historically when an early-stage company got funded, 60–80% of the capital would be used for Engineering and Development build-outs for software; that has changed dramatically. Start-ups will need less capital to actually build their products. Spending will shift to sales and marketing but those will require variable capital deployments. This means that the cost of starting a company will decrease dramatically."

There are nearly 10,000 venture capital firms globally and 3,417 VC firms in the US alone, according to the NVCA.[14] The number of venture firms in the last

---

14 NVCA, "NVCA Yearbook," https://nvca.org/nvca-yearbook, accessed 7 July 2025

COMPANY CREATION

twenty years has quadrupled. According to Statista, the worldwide VC market is forecasted to reach US$286.26 billion in 2025 with the average VC deal size being US$15 million.[15] Crunchbase estimates that close to a third of all start-ups funded in 2024 were AI companies.[16] The average VC fund size has nearly doubled in the last ten years reaching US$153.8million from only US$84million. The median seed size round of financing for a start-up has reached US$3 million as these fund sizes and their minimum check sizes have increased.

While this makes sense from a market perspective for investors (limited partners, or LPs) who have looked for outsized investment returns chasing alpha with the rise of alternative investment vehicles to increase their venture exposure, the world has changed.

AI is democratizing entrepreneurship, and the role of private investors will play a bigger and bigger role in their funding. Only 1,500 start-ups a year receive venture funding and 50,000 received angel funding in the last two years. Yet there is a glaring disequilibrium that is apparent in the VC industry and its role in funding start-ups. While VC funds have gotten larger, which meant larger fees for their managers and larger check

---

15 Statista, "Venture Capital – Worldwide," www.statista.com/outlook/fmo/capital-raising/traditional-capital-raising/venture-capital/worldwide, accessed 7 July 2025
16 G Teare, "Startup funding regained its footing in 2024 as AI became the star of the show," *Crunchbase News*, https://news.crunchbase.com/venture/global-funding-data-analysis-ai-eoy-2024, accessed 21 October 2025

sizes for the start-ups they invested in with larger valuations, AI is making it easier and cheaper to start companies that will need less capital at the application layer where many of these new AI start-ups will emerge.

According to our own research at EMG.AI, there will be over a million new AI-enabled businesses started in the next three years alone in the US. How will they be funded? How will they get the level of service and connectivity they need with buyers, or their products and services and service providers? This is an opportunity we feel new AI enabled Entrepreneur platforms, like we have built at EMG.AI, will have to provide to fill the gap.

Clearly, the role of the venture industry will need to change. Like crowdfunding, which will make it easier for personal or angel investors to invest in start-ups, so too will the fund structure need to change for the venture industry. Smaller, more nimble funds will emerge that can cut smaller check sizes while putting the entrepreneur at the center and providing services to help them succeed. Good entrepreneurs will get the fact that it will be better for them to be more efficient with capital to make better decisions for their stakeholders and their equity. They will require smaller investments and be more equity conscious.

The traditional venture model is broken as the top quartile, highest performing funds can only invest in millions. This leaves a wide gap in the earliest stages when entrepreneurs need the most help. Pre-seed and seed capital round requirements will get smaller (under US$500,000) and will require smaller fund sizes that are big on service to the entrepreneur and that are architected to deliver smaller check sizes to this new era of entrepreneurship. While the best funds have gotten bigger and bigger, leaving an opening for crowdfunding platforms to play a bigger role, there will also be a need for a new type of early stage venture firm.

This is why EMG has created EMG.VC, to fuel the stars of tomorrow who are building what Jim Collins called in his seminal book, *Good to Great* companies.[17] That is purpose-driven companies that we believe will use AI to increase their productivity and deliver a product or service better, faster, and more cheaply than ever before. These new AI-enabled businesses will be created with far fewer dollars and much bigger missions. They will require a new type of VC firm, built from the beginning with the entrepreneur and their needs in mind.

> **CASE STUDY: Highlander.AI**
>
> Highlander is one of the top thirty active RegCF equity crowdfunding platforms in the US. It was founded by brothers Chandler and Braden Kline as a side hustle for these two earnest and brilliant entrepreneurs. Over the course of four years, they

---

17 J Collins, *Good to Great: Why some companies make the leap … and others don't* (Random House Business, 2001)

> have built their company to be one of the most successful RegCF crowdfunding portals on the market. They have onboarded and worked with hundreds of entrepreneurs to get their companies funded. They call the companies they work with "issuers" and take a hands-on approach to ensure that every company on their site or portal is ready to raise capital and is legally qualified. In short, they help to take the guesswork out of it for entrepreneurs and their investors, most of which they don't even know yet. I helped to accelerate their business at EMG and find them the capital needed to grow their business. Highlander is looking at implementing AI to help them become the low cost, high-value provider in this space.

Intellectual property

Every company has IP—your own proprietary way you do what you do. The difference is whether that IP is protected. Most companies or entrepreneurs never get around to legally codifying their expertise until it's too late. You should. Finding the right attorney or online service to legally protect your IP has never been easier. When getting a patent, what used to cost tens of thousands and would take years to complete can now be accelerated through a new AI-enabled service called MyEdison.AI.

IP can protect you in the early days from larger, more established companies in your market stealing your idea. IP adds to your enterprise value literally, meaning companies that have patents filed, granted, or trademarks have anywhere between 5% and 23% higher valuations for their exits or their funding rounds.

IP and its protection help you as the entrepreneur to distinguish yourself from the market. Whether you are the first mover in your market and skating to where the puck is going or if you are in a crowded market but have an ingenious approach, having the right IP approach to your business will both protect and accelerate your path to success.

AI will accelerate the need for IP and invention protection for entrepreneurs. When the creation process is accelerated and made ubiquitous through AI, and large language models (LLMs) like ChatGPT can generate concepts, not just knowledge, how do you protect your ideas and inventions from potential competitive threats, including those coming from machines? IP, through patent protection.

It all starts with you as an entrepreneur, listing out and writing down what makes your product or service different. This is the first step that you must take to discern your strategy. Once you lay out your approach to IP for your business, you can then begin to meet with a registered IP patent attorney to see what can be protected. Once you file your patent for your unique invention(s) or you file your trademark to protect the protect names or brands you are developing for your asset, you are on your way to increasing the enterprise value of your business. I always think of IP in those two ways: as your protection, and for the asset value for your business. You're not developing your IP to litigate or sue companies that compete, you're developing your IP strategy and filing patents and trademarks so you never need to sue or litigate. It is to protect you.

When you create your company or extend your growth through innovation and new products and services, it all starts with IP. Protect it now. There is a great new service that is democratizing the IP process and which uses AI to protect the inventor, accelerate the time, and decrease the cost for entrepreneurs. MyEdison.AI was created to streamline the IP creation and protection process for entrepreneurs.

Today, there are nearly 2.5 million patent applications pending, with over 20% coming from the US alone. The average time to get a patent, according to the United States Patent and Trademark Office (USPTO), can be upwards of twenty-four months,[18] with 54% of all patents that completed the process being granted. Unfortunately, only 10% of entrepreneurs or companies complete the patent process because of the historic time, cost, and precious access to the right resources to get a patent done properly. With AI,

---

18   USPTO, "Patent FAQs," www.uspto.gov/help/patent-help#type-browse-faqs_1208, accessed 7 July 2024

COMPANY CREATION

however, the need for patent protection will accelerate, but AI will also help streamline the process with the advent of MyEdison.AI. At EMG, we believe that patent filings will grow tenfold in the next seven years as AI will accelerate entrepreneurship and the need for entrepreneurs to protect their inventions. Below is a list of common IP asset filings.[19]

Patents

A patent is a government-granted right that gives an inventor exclusive control over their invention, preventing others from making, using, or selling it for a specific period, typically twenty years. It's like a legal shield protecting an idea or innovation from being copied or used without permission. There are three primary types of patents: utility, method, and design patents.

Trademarks

A trademark can be any word, phrase, symbol, design, or a combination of these things that identifies your goods or services. It's how customers recognize you in the marketplace and distinguish you from your competitors. The word "trademark" can

---

19 USPTO, "Protecting Intellectual Property in the United States: A guide for small and medium-sized enterprises in the United Kingdom," www.uspto.gov/sites/default/files/documents/UK-SME-IP-Toolkit_FINAL.pdf, accessed 7 July 2024

refer to both trademarks and service marks. A trademark is used for goods, while a service mark is used for services.

A trademark:

- Identifies the source of your goods or services
- Provides legal protection for your brand
- Helps you guard against counterfeiting and fraud

Copyrights

A copyright is a form of protection grounded in the US Constitution and granted by law for original works of authorship fixed in a tangible medium of expression. Copyright covers both published and unpublished works. A copyright—a form of IP law—protects original works of authorship including literary, dramatic, musical, and artistic works such as poetry, novels, movies, songs, computer software, and architecture. Copyright does not protect facts, ideas, systems, or methods of operation, although it may protect the way these things are expressed.

Trade secrets

Trade secrets are IP rights on confidential information that may be sold or licensed.

Thomas Edison and the power of invention

Thomas Edison is one of the world's greatest inventors. Edison held 1,093 patents at the time of his death and helped to perfect the art of invention. He is credited with creating the lightbulb but also made incredible contributions to mass communication, sound recording, and motion pictures. He is also credited with helping to found one of the largest companies of the twentieth century, the General Electric Corporation, which was originally based on his inventions and patents. Like all of us, Edison had his challenges and went through his own hero's journey to discover his life's mission and purpose. My favorite story about Edison is the tale of his childhood and the role of his mother in protecting him and believing in him. The story goes:

One day, as a young boy, Thomas Edison came home from school and gave his mother a letter that the school had handed to him to bring home. The letter said that the school was no longer able to accept young Thomas anymore, stating he was "mentally deficient." Thomas asked his mother what was in the letter; his mother told him at the time that the letter had said, "Your son is such a genius that the school didn't have good enough teachers to teach him." Thomas's mother taught young Thomas at home, protecting and building his confidence and genius.

Edison later wrote about finding the original letter from the school after his mother passed away many years later, "Thomas Alva Edison was an addled child who by a hero mother became the genius of the century."[20]

MyEdison.AI was built in honor of Thomas Alva Edison and his mother's belief in him and in the power of invention. The mission of MyEdison.AI is to democratize IP for entrepreneurs to help protect their inventions. It's like having the power of Edison in your online pocket.

Start now. Protect yourself.

---

20 Tomhasker, "How Thomas Edison's mother was the making of him ...," *Lighthouse Global Community* (19 January 2022), www.lighthousecommunity.global/post/how-thomas-edison-s-mother-was-the-making-of-him, accessed 7 July 2025

THREE

Executing Your Company's Mission Through Action

How you lay out your organizational structure will be key to your success in building your business. You should think about your business like a great architect who lays forth the foundation of a house or building. Your pillars of business will essentially become the floor plans of your building and will provide an understanding of the functional roles you lay out. Today, with the advent of AI, it is possible that you will need fewer people to fulfill your business function needs.

Structuring your company for success

An organizational structure is based upon functional roles and how they are managed. Examples of functional roles include sales, finance, marketing, operations, and customer service or success. The old hierarchical organization has given way to a flat inversed pyramid, meaning that these roles with clear functional lines now report in a more iterative or flat manner. Some of the best organizational structures I have seen have their customer or mission in the middle with all the functions rolling into that. In the age of the "servant leader," the CEO and/or founder has moved into a role where they are seen as a leader who inspires great work rather than the traditional view of the CEO or founder having an ultimate command and control role with direct reports.

Hour-long departmental or functional review meetings have given way to brief daily stand-up meetings or as the CEO of Nvidia preaches, "direct reports with no one-to-one meetings."[21] These details will be determined by you. The first step is to imagine what kind of organizational structure you want. Will it be flat, iterative, inclusive, or something more traditional? It all begins with how you lay out your organization (or your floor plan) in your mind before you start to draw it out over the next one, two, three, or four years.

---

21   J Kahn, "60 direct reports, but no 1-on-1 meetings: How an unconventional leadership style helped Jensen Huang of Nvidia become one of the most powerful people in business," *Fortune* (12 November 2024), https://fortune.com/2024/11/12/jensen-huang-nvidia-ceo-leadership-mpp, accessed 18 August 2025

Human capital mapping

After you lay out your organizational structure in terms of the functions and roles you want to include, you will need to map out your financial projections. You will do this in your business plan or business model canvas, and you will need to think about the team you want to build and what it will stand for. When you think about what your team will stand for, you'll need to know the core values you want everyone to espouse and then find the best people you can to build out your mission and your business in a way that aligns with your goals.

As a business, an entrepreneur, and a leader, you will need to devise not just the battle plan as to how you are going to lay out your organizational structure and position people in roles across the organization but also how you're going to recruit them into your company and compensate them. I argued in my co-authored best-selling book on capitalism, *The Mission Corporation*, that you should compensate every member on your team, your advisory board, and your board of directors with not just the traditional salary and incentives plan but also with stock, via stock option grants if you are a corporation or profit-sharing interests if you are an LLC. I learned this from my own experience at Cambridge Technology Partners (CTP), a Safeguard Scientifics company where my mentor Pete Musser was chairman.

Although I was an associate consultant and programmer when I was first hired as a newly minted graduate at CTP, I felt I was part of the team, and I had a real interest in its success. The shares or stock options I got were not many, but it was the intent and culture behind giving them that meant from day one I felt part of the team. The company cared about my contribution and showed me that through their incentive stock option program. As I have said earlier, in twenty or thirty years' time our kids or grandkids won't sign up to work for a company unless it has such a plan in place.

If you are building a business, implementing a stock option is not just about being a good or decent leader, it is truly good for business. Your team will feel more part of your mission, they will care more about their work, and they will work harder with all stakeholders to fulfill your goals.

As an entrepreneur, deciding compensation and having a plan for human capital is an important aspect of managing and building your team.

Here are some tips to help you make informed decisions:

- **Research industry standards.** Start by researching what your competitors are paying their employees in similar roles. This will give you a baseline for compensation and help you stay competitive in the market. LinkedIn is a great resource to understand compensation bands. Additionally, there are many online and AI resources like FoundersGPT.AI.

- **Consider the job responsibilities.** The responsibilities of each role should be taken into consideration when determining compensation. More responsibility typically equates to higher pay, but the stage of your company will dictate what type of team member you want or need. Will they need to be in the office or totally remote? The future will be organic. Skilled specialists may need to be remote but operational execution, inside sales representatives, or sales development representatives (SDRs) will need to be in the office at least partially.

- **Look at experience and qualifications.** Experienced employees and those with higher levels of education or certifications may warrant higher pay. Younger team members might present some risk, but if you have a good "onboarding" process where team members learn about your company, its product, or service, you may not need to have experienced team members with knowledge of your industry. Whether they are young or older, new people to your market or space may not have bad habits yet. They may not think "this is how it has always been done." AI is a great democratizing force for training. Use it.

- **Assess performance.** Performance should be assessed regularly and used as a basis for determining bonuses, raises, or promotions. Your business should be a meritocracy and reward performance and the intangible contributions, which you can make tangible through performance reviews like "culture contribution." I would rather have a seven out of ten in performance and a ten in culture than a ten in performance and a seven in culture. Culture is a great thing, and a bad team member can erode it. My biggest mistakes as a leader have been keeping people too long and not helping them leave to find a place that more aligns to their particular cultural contributions.

- **Establish a compensation structure.** Having a clear compensation structure will help you make consistent and fair decisions across your organization. Make it incentive heavy to reward performance and company success. My old company used to call it a "cafeteria plan." A cafeteria plan had standard salary bands across levels (VP–director–manager–associate) with large variable pay for performance. It's a clean way to align interests and have a repeatable model for hiring and pay.

- **Create a benefits package.** In addition to salary or hourly pay, consider offering benefits such as health insurance, retirement plans, paid time off, or flexible work arrangements. When you bring somebody on board and hire them, having a package of benefits can help them mitigate risks and join you. Payroll companies offer plans that are efficient and effective for businesses of all sizes.

- **Develop a human capital plan.** This plan should outline your total pay packages, including salaries and incentives structures. Having it in place will save you time and reduce complexities and issues.

- **Establish a stock option or profit interests pool.** Typical stock option plans are for 5–10% of the total stock of a company. They are given or allocated based on the role. This pool should last for two years, meaning you won't give all 5–10% of stock out in grants because you will hold some in reserve in the pool. Also, they should be structured over a three-to-four-year vesting schedule for as long as the employee is still at your company. This means your team member only earns, say, 25% of their grant each year. If the team member leaves the company, they should forfeit all of their shares or only retain the amount they have earned over that period. This is a good way to protect you but also reward loyalty

Also, all stock options should fully vest in the event that you successfully sell the company. This is a way to align incentives for you, your team, and your shareholders. The stock options should be priced at the last round or last time the company was valued if you brought investors in. This will ensure fairness and protect the team member or employee from any tax issues they may have. The point here is that you can't grant stock options at a lower price than the value of the business at the point they received them.

Roles and responsibilities

When it comes to assessing team members and assigning roles and responsibilities, there are several best practices that small businesses in the United States can follow:

- **Clearly define the roles and responsibilities of each team member.** This can help avoid confusion and ensure that everyone understands what is expected of them. It is not just about tasks. Every team member should be on a mission with their role or job that aligns to the overall mission for your business.

- **Assess individual strengths and weaknesses.** Understanding the strengths and weaknesses of each team member can help you assign tasks that are a good fit for their skill set. This can help improve productivity and overall team performance.

- **Provide training and support.** If team members lack certain skills needed for a particular task, consider providing training and support to help them develop those skills. This can help improve overall team performance and promote growth within the organization. I argued in *The Mission Corporation* that due to the proliferation of online education, companies could offer a US$500 or US$1,000 incentive or company expense per employee for online learning to brush up on new skills. It will help your business and show your team members that you care about them and their future.

- **Communicate regularly.** Regular communication with team members can help ensure that everyone is on the same page and that tasks are being completed on time. Encourage open and honest communication to foster a culture of collaboration and accountability. Weekly one-to-one and all-hands meetings are a great tool.

- **Evaluate performance regularly.** This can help identify areas for improvement and ensure that everyone is meeting expectations. Use performance metrics and feedback to help team members understand where they stand and how they can improve. Annual performance reviews are now mandated by some clients via their compliance and governance processes. Make it a standard in your company.

Overall, managing team members' performance and their roles and responsibilities is an ongoing process that requires regular communication, evaluation, and support. By following these best practices, organizations can lead by example and show acquirers and future team members that you are not just a visionary entrepreneur but also have your stuff together as an organization and as a leader.

Board formation

Boards for companies can take many forms. You will need to form a traditional board of directors. This is a governance board of managers or stewards that will ensure your company is operating within your organization's guidelines or company articles of incorporation. Having a proper, formal, and working board shows that you don't just have a business but that you *mean* business.

Governance means upholding your organizational standards and procedures, abiding by your bylaws, and helping to manage and report to your stakeholders. This is a serious role. Traditionally, young companies may only have a board of directors of three to five people and the founder(s) will be the first members. Odd numbers are the norm to ensure board votes are carried through majority rules.

Board of director members in larger companies get paid for their participation in cash and stock options. A typical board meets quarterly, and the fourth quarter of the final board meeting of the previous year is usually used to approve the financial projections and plans for achieving the budget in the following year. Boards of directors typically carry D&O insurance policies due to their responsibility and the fear of potential lawsuits from customers or shareholders.

The board of advisers and board of directors

A new type of board is emerging for start-ups and growth-oriented companies of all kinds: the board of advisers. Boards of advisers do not have governance responsibilities. They can serve to help your business grow through generating new introductions or for suggesting growth ideas to help shape your product or manufacturing roadmaps. These advisers are typically compensated through commissions or stock option grants that reward involvement. This is a great new tool to help your business grow.

Forming an advisory board and board of directors can be a crucial step in building a successful small business. An advisory board can provide guidance and insight, while a board of directors can offer strategic oversight and decision-making authority.

Here are some steps to take when forming a proper and functioning board:

- **Define the purpose and objective of each board.** With your dream board in mind, determine what role the advisory board and board of directors will play in the company and what specific responsibilities each group will have. What would each board do? What type of people would be in each one? How would you work with each of the boards to help your business grow?

- **It's all about the people.** Look for individuals with relevant expertise and experience who can contribute valuable insights, advice, and connectivity, with introductions to help your business grow. Most importantly, make sure the people you choose align with your purpose or vision. Consider individuals from diverse backgrounds and perspectives to provide a broad range of input and add value to your vision for the company.

- **Define roles and responsibilities.** Clearly outline the roles and responsibilities of each board member, including any expectations for meetings, participation in decision making, and communication with other members. Set expectations early.

- **Establish meeting frequency and structure.** Determine how often the boards will meet and how the meetings will be structured. Consider whether meetings will be in-person, virtual, or a combination of both.

- **Reward board members.** Set up a compensation and benefits plan on how they will be rewarded. Determine whether board members will be paid or receive any other benefits, such as stock options or equity. Highly incentivized board or advisory board members are the most engaged and aligned.

- **Develop bylaws and governance documents.** These should outline the structure, roles, and responsibilities of each board member. Formalization shows professionalism and alignment.

Overall, forming an advisory board and board of directors can be an important step in building a successful small business. These groups can provide valuable guidance and oversight to help the business grow and thrive.

Planning and formatting

I always use both a 1000-day and a 100-day plan to operate my businesses because they aren't too long and they help to flesh out the important actions my team and I need to nail down and get done to get buy-in. Napoleon had a 1000-day battle plan or may have had the seed of this idea. As the great business strategist Pete Drucker said, "You can't manage what you don't measure."

100-day plan

The 100-day plan is a great format and template that focuses on execution and deliverables by you and your team. They are self-measuring, meaning you have to stick to your goals and objectives, which will reward action. 100-day plans cover roughly a quarter (or three months) and are magic for execution; they are terrific planning mechanisms or tools that help you align what is important in the short term to accomplish your business goals. They are also cross-functional—dependent on other parts of your company where you may not control all the executables.

Here is an example of one format that I use:

FUNCTION	30 DAYS	60 DAYS	90 DAYS	OWNER
📊				
📢				
🤝				
⚙️				
💬				
👥				
⚖️				
Totals				

Example of a 100-day business plan

1000-day plan

A 1000-day plan is a three-plus-year look that should align to your financial pro forma projections. 1000-day plans are ambitious and should map to the vision you have of your business. This is an aggressive and optimistic view of what your business would look like if you "run the table," as they say, and accomplish everything you want or dream of because your business has met interested revenue goals.

By function or department:

- What milestones would you reach?
- How many clients would you serve?
- How many users would you have?
- What would your product or service look like?
- What would it be capable of?
- What would your business valuation be?

A 1000-day business planning template is a comprehensive outline of the objectives and strategies for a business to be achieved within the next three years. The template includes an overview of the current status of the business, future growth projections, and the steps needed to achieve these goals. Your 1000-day plan should be time based over those 1000 days, based upon your organization and departmental goals and strategy.

A 1000-day business planning template should contain:

- **Executive summary.** A brief summary of the overall plan, including goals and objectives, target market, competitive landscape, and financial projections for your business.

- **Current status assessment.** An analysis of the current status of the business, including strengths, weaknesses, opportunities, and threats (SWOT). This section should also include a SWOT analysis and market research data. Such an analysis lays out the strengths, weaknesses, opportunities, and threats in four quadrants of a company and its products or services. It is usually created by the founding or executive team of the company and should be objective based upon market feedback from prospects, clients, or your competitive set.

- **Vision and mission outcomes.** A clear statement of the company's vision and mission, and how these align with the overall goals of the business. Your business purpose will be your true north and should be represented in everything you do.

- **Long-term objectives and outcomes.** Think with your end in mind. Start with a list of the key objectives and accomplishments for the business over the next 1000 days, including financial, marketing, operational, and customer service goals. Where would you be on that journey? How many goals would be fulfilled? Start with your goals and objectives in mind and work backward.

- **Growth strategy and outcome.** A detailed plan for achieving the long-term objectives, including marketing and sales strategies, product development, and customer acquisition plans. How will you execute? What would success look like for your business?

- **Competitive landscape and outcome.** An analysis of the competition, including their strengths and weaknesses, market share, and potential threats to the business. How much market share would you or your competitors have? What would your competitive set look like by then, and by what time would they appear? Often, your biggest competitor is not in your market today. Think about how your market will evolve and grow and where you fit.

- **Marketing strategy and outcomes.** A detailed plan for promoting the business and its products or services, including target market analysis, advertising and promotional campaigns, and social media strategies. Where would your ads be running? How many leads would you have brought in and by what channel? Would you have an article in *Forbes* or one million subscribers to your newsletter? How many followers do you have on social media?

- **Sales strategy and outcomes.** A plan for increasing sales and revenue, including lead generation tactics, customer acquisition strategies, and sales forecasting. Where would you be? How many customers would you serve? How many salespeople or SDRs would you have? What would your booked revenue be? How about your pipeline? Would you have distributors? If so, how many? Who would they be?

- **Operations plan and outcomes.** A plan for managing the day-to-day operations of the business, including staffing, workflow management, and quality control. How big would your organization be? How many people? What systems or processes would you have in place?

- **Financial projections.** A detailed financial plan, including revenue projections, expenses, cash flow analysis, and profit and loss statements. Pro forma creation is critical for planning and for your ability to paint the picture to investors on how your business will evolve and grow and the capital requirements you may need.

- **Risk management plan.** An assessment of the potential risks to the business, including financial, operational, and reputational risks, and a plan for managing and mitigating these risks. What risks do you see in your business in the future? How would they be mitigated or not?

Product roadmapping

The product roadmap is your plan for product or service innovation to continually improve your product and service. It is your architectural rendering or bible for where your product or service is today and where it is going. The product roadmap is made up of features (smaller product or service improvements) as well as functions or functionality (larger product enhancements or improvements in terms of capabilities for your clients and users). Those features and functions are prioritized and mapped out.

The priorities are usually based on the following criteria:

- **Investment in time or resources.** How long and how much will it cost per feature or functionality?
- **Business bang or revenue generation.** Will the feature bring in more revenue?
- **Customer retention.** Will the new feature or functionality increase your customer success or retention rate with existing customers? Will it help them stay longer as a client?
- **Innovation versus competitors.** Will this new feature or functionality increase your competitive advantage?

- **Brand equity.** Will this new feature or functionality increase the value of your brand?

EXERCISE: Product functional mapping

Use this template as a starting point to map your and weight your product functionality to ensure proper prioritization. This should not be a static, one-time exercise, but a continually evolving procedure which adds real value to your business by ensuring continued product or service enterprise value creation for your business.

	Customer retention	Increase revenue	Competitive advantage	Brand equity	
Weight	30%	40%	20%	10%	Score
Feature or functionality 1					
Feature or functionality 2					
Feature or functionality 3					
Feature or functionality 4					
Feature or functionality 5					
Feature or functionality 6					

EXECUTING YOUR COMPANY'S MISSION THROUGH ACTION

Your product roadmap

Success comes when you lay out your ideas and create a plan around product enhancements. Create a spreadsheet and have columns next to each of your planned product enhancements stating the five key criteria items for each product.

You should then have team meetings to assign a rating (one to ten) on each component and then weight the components as to their importance to your goals. This means, for example, that revenue generation may be weighted at 50% and brand equity only 10% so those one to ten rankings will have more meaning for the highest prioritized goal.

Your product roadmap should be a living breathing document, driven by your CTO or head of product. The weekly or monthly meetings to review the product roadmap should be cross-functional, with department or team leaders all participating in them. The CEO and CTO or head of product should have the final say, but it is important to get everyone's input and buy-in into the process.

As a real-life example, The Code Registry (www.thecoderegistry.com) is a London-based AI software company that my company EMG has advised, signed, and invested in. It was created by its genius Co-Founder and CTO Stephen Grey and led from a business perspective by Co-Founder Mark Purdy. The Code

Registry is the first-ever AI-enabled Software as a Service (SaaS) company of its kind. It helps CXOs to understand what their code does, how it works, how and who created it, what it is worth, and how AI can assist in the future to streamline development.

Every company today, in one way or another, is a software company because they all have software assets such as websites, portals, applications, or third-party developed or hosted software applications. In a sense, this demystifies software code. Since The Code Registry's business is literally software enabling every leader of any company around the world to "know their code," their product roadmap is critical to their company's success.

When The Code Registry was starting out, they were lucky to have a minimal viable product (MVP) demonstration of how the software could work and what it would do. They did this via a working prototype but also via mocked-up screens to show the user experience. When they presented to my club, The Mission Capitalist Club (www.MissionCapitalist.Club), they were able to not only go through their presentation or pitch deck to potential investors but they also showed in detail their product roadmap as to where they were going to go with the product.

This level of detail and their ability to articulate it in terms of their wider mission and purpose, which was to help democratize code knowledge to every CXO in the world, won them the day. They were oversubscribed, and investors were excited and flocked to them. They were passionate, detailed, and clear as to their mission and where the product was going to go. The Code Registry Roadmap took the form creatively of the structure I presented above. It made the difference to their ability to not just tell their story but show with belief and executional detail where they were going. Today, the company has executed on their product roadmap, and the product is successfully in the market with many users and a large pipeline of potential contracts and clients.

3-2-1 mission activation

After your family, your business will be the other purpose of your life as an entrepreneur. Your business is your professional mission. It is the way, as Steve Jobs says, that you can put a "dent in the universe." Your business is an instrument that can change what can be. It's your canvas to create the life you want to be known for to yourself, your family, your team, your investors, and the clients you serve. Structurally, you can create this not just by having a mission for your business beyond the dollars and cents of what you help to make but in how you will impart that success to others or your community.

We created a way to embed the mission into your company's DNA or fabric early in the creation process, or in the growth phase of your business. The 3-2-1 mission activation method is a strategic approach to setting and achieving goals in your small business.

Here are some tips on how you can implement the 3-2-1 mission:

- **Set your mission.** Start by defining the mission for your business, which outlines the purpose and objectives beyond dollars and cents. What are you really doing? If your business was huge and successful, what will it be able to do? Who do you want to serve and how? What is your *why*

  The mission of EMG.AI, my new AI Venture Platform company, is to democratize entrepreneurship globally by helping over a million entrepreneurs create and build businesses that change their lives and everyone they touch or serve.

- **Write your mission statement.** Your mission statement should be big, ambitious, clear, concise, and aligned with your values and long-term vision. It should be something that, when the chips are down (and they will be at times), inspires you to get up in the morning and go forward. It should be where you show how what you are doing will change the lives of who you serve.

- **Write your mission objectives.** Put your 3-2-1 mission objectives down and in action in your organization documents or in your unofficial or official company charter or handbooks. It should state that your business will contribute 3% of employee or team member time to charities or community efforts that your company is passionate about; 2% of net income to these same causes or charities that inspire your team; and 1% of your stock option pool or revenue toward these same charities or causes.

I argued in *The Mission Corporation* that the way mission capital works is not a leftist or progressive way of thinking about business or capitalism but is actually an ideology of true conservatism, as my Scottish friend Guy Robertson would agree. Adam Smith, the great economist and philosopher, knew this and wrote about it in his book, *The Wealth of Nations*.[22] It is not just the right thing to do but it also makes for good business to work in this way.

---

22 A Smith, *The Wealth of Nations* (Independently published, 2023)

FOUR
Positioning Your Business For Success

In the early days of my career, the first thing I did when I was brought in as an executive or when building my own company was to start a fresh new company presentation. This—our mission deck—would tell the story and the purpose of what we were doing and what we were offering.

Many investors, investment bankers, and successful entrepreneurs have their own secret recipe or format for their desired presentation flow or deck. It is important that you make it your own and you do one thing many founders don't do well enough: to focus on the *why*. The why is usually where your mission comes from. It will distinguish you from others in your market or space and is where the magic lives for you and for your business. It is where the passion resides, which will show through when you present your deck.

How to build your mission deck

I have found that the best way to lay out your deck is in the following format:

1. **Title slide:** Your logo and tagline.
2. **Mission slide:** What are you doing?
3. **Why slide:** Your purpose for doing it. Why are you different?
4. **Market slide:** The market you are in. What is the market sizing?
5. **Competition slide:** Who are your competitors? (Use a grid layout or landscape slide.)
6. **Product or service slides:** How you are doing what you do. Why are you different? What is your IP or invention?
7. **Business model:** How you will make money doing it. What is your pricing and why?
8. **Go-to-market slide:** How you will be marketing it and getting the word out. For example, is it a freemium model or is it driven by online marketing?

9. **Pro forma:** Your three-to-five-year financial projections. Usually two slides: one showing financial projections (in Excel format imported into a slide) and a slide of financial projections/growth showing your trajectory (a line or bar chart).

10. **Team slide:** Who is your founding and/or management team? Use pictures and bios (one to two lines for each).

11. **Board and advisers slide:** Who is following you into your journey and helping you by providing guidance?

12. **Terms slide:** If it is an investor deck, add your investment terms.

13. **Client slide:** If instead of an investor deck it is a customer pitch, add the client logo and explain your ideas on how they can use your product or service to make them even more successful in three to five bullet points.

The slide presentation deck for your company (sometimes referred to as your pitch deck) should be no more than twenty four slides and no fewer than sixteen. Key items of consideration besides killer content will be to make it engaging and personal with great creatives and graphics that show the depth of your mission and belief in what you are doing, as well as your professionalism as an organization. We like the idea of utilizing an approach when presenting and thinking through your slide-deck presentation around the concept of the 4 P's.

- **Purpose:** What is the purpose of your business? As the great Simon Sinek says, "What is your why?" This should be your guiding force that will set your business and your pitch apart.[23]

- **Potential:** What is the potential or the Total Addressable Market (TAM) of the market you are going to compete in? Investor, partners, customers, or acquirers want to hear how big the market is.

- **Product:** What about your product or service, is it unique to the market? How is your product or service better, faster, or cheaper than other competitors in your space?

- **People:** Finally, who are the people behind your company? Why are you or your team perfect for this mission?

Sales expansion, recruiting, and strategy

The first company I worked for after college was an amazing technology and management consulting firm called CTP, which had a world-class management team. During their new employee orientation, I remember vividly that their EVP of worldwide marketing and the legendary technology marketer from

---

23   S Sinek, *Start With Why* (Penguin, 2025)

Oracle, Christopher Greendale, had us all stand up and raise our hands when he asked forty new programmers and consultants in the room, "Who is in sales here?" What Chris made us all understand was that every single person—regardless of whether they were coding software for clients or facilitating management consulting engagements—was, in fact, in sales. Every action taken by an employee was an element of the sales process.

Sales is essential to *every* business; without sales, there would be no business. Chris had a great line that he and his VP of marketing would often share, "Marketing is sales with a degree." By this he meant that good marketing set the product and company strategy on which sales could then be made.

In companies, too often sales are relegated to a department. To truly create an enduring mission-driven business, *everyone* should be in sales. The sales department should be like a group of Navy SEALs (the elite group that the US Navy brings to battle). Salespeople are the sharp shooters and stalwarts of any offense that the company brings to the game, every game.

Today, with advancements in technology, sales can take many forms. They can be online, driven through integrated marketing. Traditional sales from a departmental perspective now need to be equipped with knowledge of how the internet and AI helps to make the sales process more efficient.

The sales department of the future has many different structures and roles, but typically it falls into these three categories:

1. **Create an engine room with presales with SDRs.** Early software companies, when software was a longer sales cycle, had presales engineers. They were the geniuses that made the product demonstration work. Manufacturing companies tend to still use this structure, but today that role has morphed into SDRs—those great people that help to book meetings online, by phone, or using AI technology for the sales team to close. These are often entry-level positions for people who are breaking into new companies or industries. They utilize CRM tools such as Salesforce and other technologies, as well as social media channels and avenues like LinkedIn, to get the message out there for the company and sales team.

   The ratio for these roles is typically one-to-one or two-to-one, meaning for every one SDR there would be one salesperson that would receive these warm leads. These individuals usually have a smaller base salary, especially when compared to direct sales, but can earn anywhere from 20% to 40% of inventive compensation, in the form of commissions for meetings booked or deals closed, for their direct sales team member.

2. **Direct sales.** This is the role that most often comes to mind when we think of sales. These

are salaried-plus-commission individuals who carry a quota (sales goals) for the organization and are rewarded handsomely when the product or service sells. Their roles are often in-house, but now, more than ever, people work in these roles remotely. Direct salespeople are responsible for closing accounts and ensuring customers are contracted properly. These individuals typically have compensation that is 60% salary and 40% incentive compensation or commission. Commission rates, depending on the industry, can range from 5% all the way to 20%.

3. **Account management or business development.** In early stage companies, account management and account success are often done by the direct sales leader. In years two or three, as businesses enter their growth stage, this function is usually broken out.

   A great account manager handles larger accounts to service and upsell them. Often, they become business development managers that help to establish important partnerships to create a one-to-many relationship for your business.

   An example of this would be a company that sells a product that could benefit from an ecosystem or channel that could create a ten-times change in growth for product distribution. Account managers typically have 80–90% of their compensation in the form of the salary versus a bonus structure.

Recruiting salespeople

Deciding whether to recruit a salesperson for your business depends on several factors such as the complexity of your product or service, your target market, and your business goals. If your product or service requires in-depth knowledge and explanation, a dedicated salesperson may be necessary. Additionally, if your target market is large and requires a lot of outreach, a salesperson can help you reach potential customers.

When it comes to recruiting a salesperson, there are several steps you can take:

1. **Define the role.** Before recruiting, define the role you want the salesperson to play. What will their responsibilities be? What skills and experience do they need to have? What will their goals and targets be?

2. **Create a job description.** Based on the role definition, create a job description that outlines the responsibilities, requirements, and qualifications for the position.

3. **Identify where to recruit.** You can recruit salespeople from various sources such as online job boards, LinkedIn, industry events, or through referrals.

4. **Screen résumés and applications.** Review résumés and applications to identify the most qualified candidates.

5. **Conduct interviews.** Conduct phone or in-person interviews to further assess the candidates' skills, experience, and fit for the role.

6. **Evaluate candidates.** Evaluate the candidates' skills, experience, and fit for the role to determine the best fit for your business.

7. **Make an offer.** Once you have identified the best candidate, make an offer and negotiate compensation and benefits.

Recruiting a salesperson is not a one-time process. You should continue to evaluate and train your sales team to ensure they are meeting your business goals and objectives.

Brand voice/advertising

Your brand is the feeling someone has when they hear your company's name or see your product or service. Brands take time to build. The soul of your brand is its voice in the market: the feeling it invokes, the content you produce, the colors you use, the logo you create, and the tagline that supports your mission.

Brand guidelines are important for any business, regardless of its size or industry. They provide a clear, consistent way for your brand to be presented to the public and ensure that everyone involved in creating and promoting your brand understands the appropriate use of your logo, colors, fonts, tone of voice, and other visual and messaging elements. Having brand guidelines helps to establish brand recognition and loyalty, which can lead to increased customer engagement, sales, and overall success. They also help to protect your brand by ensuring that it is presented accurately and consistently across all channels and touchpoints.

If you're just starting out or have a small business, you may not need a comprehensive set of brand guidelines but it's still important to establish some basic guidelines and standards for your brand. This can include things like your logo usage, color palette, and tone of voice. As your business grows, you can continue to refine and expand your brand guidelines.

Creating brand guidelines can be done in-house or with the help of a branding or design agency. The key is to ensure that your guidelines are clear, comprehensive, and accessible to everyone involved in your brand's creation and promotion.

Business process functional mapping

Every business has a set of processes or execution steps across each function and for everything they do. Sales has a function and a set of steps or business processes from lead to contracting to closing. The same holds true with customer service or success, technology or product, finance and administration, and operations.

What I have found useful is to lay out across functional areas those steps that get done for the function to exist and be effective. A plane always has a "black box," and similarly, every business has too. That black box is the set of functional business processes that have to get done in order for their representative tasks to be completed or that department or function to flourish. Why not codify those steps early on and continually refine and document them so that your business could outlast you. We call this idea "business process functional mapping."

Business process functional mapping is the process of documenting and analyzing the steps involved in completing a specific task or process within a business. This helps to identify areas for improvement, streamline processes, and ensure consistency and efficiency.

There are several reasons why you should consider doing business process functional mapping for your business. They include:

- **Identifying inefficiencies.** Mapping out your business processes can help you identify areas where tasks are taking too long, too many people are involved, or there are other inefficiencies that can be addressed.

- **Increasing productivity.** By streamlining your business processes, you can reduce the time and effort required to complete tasks, freeing up your employees to focus on other areas of the business.

- **Improving customer service.** Mapping out your business processes can help you identify areas where customer service can be enhanced, such as by reducing wait times or improving response times.

- **Ensuring consistency.** By documenting your business processes, you can ensure that everyone in your organization is following the same procedures, reducing errors and ensuring consistency.

To do business process functional mapping:

1. **Select a process that you want to map out.** For example, onboarding new employees or fulfilling customer orders.

2. **Break down each step involved in completing that process.** Include who is responsible for each step and how long it takes to complete. You can use tools such as flowcharts, process maps, or swim lane diagrams to help visualize the process.

3. **Review the process with your team.** Look for areas where improvements can be made. You may need to make changes to the process, such

POSITIONING YOUR BUSINESS FOR SUCCESS

as adding new or eliminating unnecessary steps to make it more efficient and effective.

This process should be worked out in a living document, such as in Google Docs or Slack, where it can be shared with your team members. Maybe choose each department head—or better, a person that exhibits great leadership potential—and put them in charge of maintaining this document as the processes become more refined over time.

It's like "AI-ing" yourself. One day many of these functions could or will be assisted by an AI agent who will manufacture actionable knowledge. The best way to start is to identify them and populate those business processes. If you do this, you will be ahead of the game. Operationally, this is where companies like yours can truly get the benefit of beginning to enable an "agentic enterprise." SoTechnology.AI utilizes a business process, user, and data flow technique to then overlay AI agents or enable these processes to become agentic to increase operational efficiency. It starts with mapping out where you are today by function and flow.

EXERCISE: Business process flow mapping

This comprehensive framework maps seven sequential process steps across six core business functions, providing a structured approach to visualizing workflows and identifying interdependencies. Each function—finance, sales, marketing, customer success, product, and operations—follows the same seven-step progression, enabling cross-functional alignment and process optimization. Use this matrix to document current site processes, identify bottlenecks, plan improvements, or onboard new team members to organizational workflows.

Function	Step 1	Step 2	Step 3	Step 4	Step 5	Step 6	Step 7 (Result)
Finance							
Sales							
Marketing							
Customer success							
Product							
Operations							

This matrix serves as a living document that evolves with your organization. Populate each cell with specific activities, milestones, or deliverables relevant to your business context. The standardized seven-step structure ensures consistency while allowing flexibility for each function's unique processes. Regular reviews of this mapping can reveal opportunities for automation, resource reallocation, and enhanced collaboration between departments.

Distinctive competency mapping

One of the greatest books ever written about business was called *The Discipline of Market Leaders*.[24] In this book, the authors laid forth their thesis that every great company has one specific competency or thing that they do better than anyone else. It could be having the best product, being the lowest cost producer or deliverer, or their attention to customer success. No one company or leader, they argued, could be all things to all people.

The adage that has been used over the past ten years in the technology sector is the idea of being "better, faster, or cheaper." This idea or concept was born from the seminal work behind this book.

EXERCISE: Distinctive competency mapping

This is important to do early on so you know what you stand for and what your brand and product will be known for. Start by laying out the market you compete in and putting down your company's or products' inherent strengths. Map those strengths against your competitors and put them on a scale from zero to ten. This will serve as your distinctive competency that can live on in all other sales and marketing presentations. It will be your Gartner Group Magic Quadrant that

---

24 M Treacy and F Wiersema, *The Discipline of Market Leaders: Choose your customers, narrow your focus, dominate your market* (Basic Books, 1997)

you have created on why your offering is unique to your competitive set. Gartner Group made this format famous and is a market leading research firm.

Strategic partnering

Alex Ott, the old head of partnerships from the great software company SAP, once said (I paraphrase): we might have 1,000 sales executives or account managers, but with our strategic partner network we have 100,000.

Strategic partnering is the development of an ecosystem or network of potential influencers or resellers for your product. Most times this costs no money. The network or ecosystem of partners get compensated based upon the number of sales they bring to your company. Strategic partnering creates a network effect for your business. It's a way for you to reach thousands or millions of users or clients through an unpaid sales force. The age of the internet, and now AI, makes this more available and even more important than ever.

Strategic partnering involves identifying and building relationships with other businesses or organizations that can help your business achieve its goals. This can include strategic alliances, joint ventures, or partnerships with suppliers, distributors, or other organizations that can provide complementary products or services.

Strategic partner analysis

To develop a strategic partnering plan for your business, begin by conducting a thorough analysis of your business and the market in which you operate. You can use many AI tools to help you research your market. You should lay out the universe of organizations or resellers or influencers your product or service can touch before it gets to your end consumer.

Doing this exercise with your board of advisers or directors can open the avenues of influence for you and your business. Introductions to potential partners in this way can hugely accelerate them coming on board.

Strategic positioning plan

Once you've completed your strategic partner analysis, you can develop a strategic positioning plan that outlines your target market, unique value proposition, and key messaging. You can also develop a distinctive competency map that identifies your unique strengths and capabilities and shows how they can be leveraged to create a competitive advantage.

Create a plan that develops materials and messaging as if you were them. In other words, why would that firm or person want to partner with you? What will they receive? Why is your product, service, or mission superior? Get them on board and build a network or ecosystem of evangelists. We have found much success with this process with one of our portfolio companies, The Code Registry. The Code Registry formed an advisory board of industry leaders who have now opened dozens of doors for the company to resell their "AI Code Intelligence" platform to a host of potential resellers and one day most likely acquirers.

Overall, developing a strategic partnering plan can help you create a clear and effective business strategy that can drive growth and success over the long term.

Recruiting talent

Human capital—the people on your team that are unique in their ability to be a market leader in your space—is the most important element of your business after your mission and reason for being. Human capital is based upon the ability for your company to acquire and retain talented team members that can help your business grow.

Recruiting talent for your business can be a challenging task but there are several steps you can take to make the process more effective. Here are some tips on how to recruit talent for your business:

1. **Define and post your mission.** Talent wants to be with people and an organization that is doing more than selling a product or service. Talent

wants to join a mission or movement that could be a billion-dollar idea or company or change the lives of billions of people. People want a mission. What is yours?

2. **Define and develop the job position.** Identify the skills, knowledge, and experience required for the role. Develop a clear, concise job description that includes the job title, responsibilities, required qualifications, and compensation details.

3. **Post the job listing everywhere.** Advertise on relevant job boards, social media, and your company website.

4. **Network.** Reach out to your network, your advisory board of relationships, industry associations, and other professionals to identify potential candidates.

5. **Review résumés and cover letters.** Identify candidates who meet the required qualifications.

6. **Conduct live or Zoom interviews.** Conduct initial phone or video interviews to determine if the candidate is a good fit for the position. See what you are looking for in your people's eyes. Make sure the people you want to bring into your company reflect your values and passions.

7. **Conduct reference checks.** Do the background legwork. Conduct reference checks to verify

the candidate's employment history, skills, and qualifications.

8. **Make a job offer to the selected candidate.** Treat them like a NBA, NFL, or Premier League player. Sell not just the salary but the package.

9. **Onboard the new employee.** Provide them with the necessary training and support to ensure they are successful in their new role.

Recruiting talent is evergreen. Even if you're not currently hiring, it's important to build relationships with potential candidates and maintain a strong employer brand to attract top talent when you need it.

To attract top talent, follow these tips:

- **Think as if you are the talent being recruited.** What is cool or unique about your company? The market: are you in AI? The location or work flexibility? The mission of what you are doing?

- **Use all avenues for distribution.** Think outside the box as to how to get the word out you are looking for talent – schools, internship programs, community and or entrepreneurial of tech groups.

- **Ask your advisers for help.** When you form an advisory board in the early days (or even later days), each person sometimes doubles or triples your own network.

- **Create an incentive program.** Offer an equity kicker (addition) or bonus to any team member, advisory board member, friend, or board member if they help you recruit talent.

- **Use LinkedIn.** I have found in twenty-five years of building teams that LinkedIn is an incredible resource for any company looking to add talent. With AI they are profiling and serving up the talent ads in a deliberate way.

- **Get an article in a local publication on your business.** Old-fashioned public relations can help you create buzz for your business and make it attractive for people wanting to join your team.

FIVE
Scoreboarding Your Business

As my friend Daniel Priestley has said brilliantly in his best-selling book, *24 Assets*, "income follows assets."[25] Daniel has identified twenty-four major business assets that entrepreneurs should think about when building their businesses. He shows you how to develop your ecosystem of assets and how to think about building them.

Assets explained

An asset is anything that would still be valuable without you. This is an important idea as it teaches you to

---

25 D Priestley, *24 Assets: Create a digital, scalable, valuable and fun business that will thrive in a fast changing world* (Rethink Press, 2017)

create, build, and think about exiting your business from the outset. Thinking about your business in this way enables you to create a much more valuable one.

The classifications and breakdowns that Dan prescribes to help you think about the assets you may have, or that you could develop as an entrepreneur, include things like IP, brand, market, products, systems, culture, and funding assets.

AI will accelerate the need for patent and IP protection as never before. AI models will share ideas, making them liquid. The differentiator will be who owns the IP and whether it's defensible. Like castles in feudal societies had moats and drawbridges to protect them from intruders and enemies, entrepreneurs' castles—their businesses—will need to build moats of IP to protect them from threats.

Here is a list of some potential assets and their classifications based upon Daniel's method:

- **Funding assets:** The business is able to raise capital or borrow money on better terms than its competitors.
  - Business plan
  - Valuation
  - Structure
  - Risk mitigation

- **Culture assets:** The business is able to attract, retain, develop, and manage great people at a lower cost than its competitors.
    - Key people of influence: management and admin
    - Marketing and sales
    - Technicians

- **Systems assets:** The business has a set of systems and processes that allow it to run more efficiently than its rivals, while still delivering the same or better quality.
    - Marketing and sales
    - Management and admin
    - Operations

- **Product assets:** The business has created unique products and services that are either difficult to replicate or to compete with.
    - Gifts
    - Product for prospects (P4P)
    - Core product
    - Products for clients (P4C)

- **Market assets:** The business can sell products, disseminate ideas, or be present to a large group of potential buyers faster and more cheaply than others in the same market.

- Position
- Channels
- Data

- **Brand assets:** The business is known, liked, and trusted by a loyal group of fans who are unlikely to switch to a new brand.

    - Philosophy
    - Identity
    - Ambassadors

- **IP assets:** The business lays claim to—or is known for—valuable ideas, methods, or defensible IP rights.

    - Content
    - Methodology
    - Registered IP (trademarks, patents, copyrights, and trade secrets)

One of the most important assets for your business by entrepreneurs is around IP. This is unfortunately often overlooked because entrepreneurs don't think they have the money to set out some sort of IP protection and documentation.

When building BizEquity, IP was one of the first things I made sure to prioritize before launching our product to democratize business valuation knowledge for small business owners and entrepreneurs. Having those trademarks, patents pending, and inventions gave me the confidence to pitch to large potential partners, like Dun & Bradstreet, Experian, and Equifax—the big three of business data.

The idea behind the "registered" assets Dan mentions are for trademarks, copyrights, or patents for your product(s) or services or other forms of protectable IP. This was one of the most important assets to develop early but often the most overlooked based upon the costs entrepreneurs think it will involve. If you can afford to get your site or app up, you should invest the little it may cost over the next year to file your invention.

Today, there is an easier way. MyEdison.AI helps any entrepreneur speed up the development and protection of their own IP to protect their invention. Having IP will protect you and help you to be confident when you are pitching to new clients and prospects, recruiting new team members, or telling strategic partners or influencers that what you are doing is novel and you have a real potential competitive advantage in the future.

Completing an asset assessment with IP blueprinting is an important process for small businesses and entrepreneurs to determine the value of their assets.

I used to get my CTO or head of engineering in a room with me and I would lead a brainstorming session around where our product was today, where it was going, and any gaps in the market where we could really disrupt it and invent innovations to potentially patent.

Locally, we had a great IP counsel who I had met through the creation of and investment in multiple companies. I would email my notes to him, ask to access the viability of getting a patent approved, and discuss the filing process and cost estimates with him. This wouldn't happen for many entrepreneurs who did not have access to cost-effective and accessible attorneys. Along with this process, as a former marketer I would write down a series of product names or taglines for each invention and in parallel file trademarks for those words or phrases. This assessment and process helps you to make informed decisions about managing your assets and gain buy-in from your core team, while making important financial decisions that can drive your asset value and thus your enterprise value for your business.

The first step in asset assessment is to identify and categorize all the assets that your business owns, or is developing, as you launch or grow your product or service line. This may include physical assets such as buildings, equipment, and inventory, products you have or are developing, as well as intangible assets such as your process, methodology, or the patents, trademarks, and IP you may already have.

Once all assets have been identified, it is important to determine their current value and forecast their potential future value. Often, you can forecast their value based upon assumptions of market usage or how they could be leveraged by a competitor that may already have a tendential product or service. This can be done through various methods such as market value, replacement cost, or income approach.

After assessing the value of your assets, you can then make decisions on how to manage them. This may include strategies such as investing in new equipment, disposing of unused assets, or protecting IP.

Capital raising

Fundraising and capital raising, while difficult to do in the earliest stages, are essential for small businesses to grow and expand.

Investors in the early stages will place a bet on you as an entrepreneur, the idea or the why, the market, and your ability to execute on your business plan or model. It is often said that investors in private businesses have a "herd mentality"—like cattle or sheep, they tend to gather around an idea or business that others are flocking to and investing in. That's why you should raise more capital than you think you need.

Larry Ellison, the iconic founder and executive chairman of Oracle, has always said that technology "is the only industry that is more fashion-driven than women's fashion."[26] Trends are fast and wide-spreading, and investors—like prospects and clients—don't want to be left behind if your product or service represents something that is part of a larger trend. Like fashion, trends in the market change quickly. My old boss Pete Musser, during his illustrious career spanning technology investment over fifty years, would change the markets he would invest in every seven to ten years based upon the market's evolution and trends in the technology industry. Pete "rode the wave" as an investor just like a surfer would in the ocean.

Every entrepreneur and emerging business in the world could use and deploy more capital to help grow their business's top-line revenue or accelerate their product or services' capability and innovation. Unfortunately, only around 12,000 businesses a year are funded by venture capitalists or private equity investors. The opportunity to get your business funded will become democratized, thanks to the innovation of AI and the disruption of the internet. This will allow the best ideas and entrepreneurs to be better seen by investors and policies, and technology access that will allow investors to find and invest in them.

Historically, for the last thirty years since the advent of the internet, fundraising has been episodic, i.e.

---

26 J Nunns, "He said what? 5 things Larry Ellison actually said about cloud," *Tech Monitor* (27 April 2015), www.techmonitor.ai/hardware/cloud/he-said-what-5-things-larry-ellison-actually-said-about-cloud-4563323, accessed 13 August 2025

based upon some laid-out timeline around milestones and the depletion of cash or capital. In the Age of AI, this model is now overdone and antiquated. Fundraising for your business should be evergreen, or "always-on." Thanks to new crowdfunding legislation in the US and soon around the world, this could be a reality for every entrepreneur globally.

Capital and fundraising come in many shapes and sizes and there are different types and processes. Here are some tips and strategies for raising capital for your small business in the US:

- **Self-funding.** One of the easiest ways to raise capital is to use your own savings or borrow from family and friends. This is known as self-funding or bootstrapping. You will be surprised at how creative you can get when it is your own money you're using.

- **Crowdfunding.** This allows you to raise funds from a large number of people via popular online platforms such as Highlander.AI, FounderStudio. AI, Kickstarter, Indiegogo, and GoFundMe. Crowdfunding is here to stay and will only grow larger as new regulations are passed and AI enables you to reach more and more potential investors, customers, and networks to help grow your value. Crowdfunding will help to democratize early stage investing that was traditionally only for LPs—wealthy private investors, endowments, or funds of VC firms.

- **Grants.** There are many grants available for small businesses in the US. You can search for grants through the Small Business Administration (SBA) website or through private organizations. SBA loans in the US are typically used by manufacturing or asset-heavy businesses that are looking to build a plant or manufacturing line or purchase a building.

- **Bank loans.** You can approach banks or other financial institutions for loans to fund your business. You will need to provide detailed financial information and a business plan to secure a loan.

- **Angel investors.** These are wealthy individuals who invest in start-ups or small businesses in exchange for equity. You can find angel investors through networking events, angel groups, or online platforms such as AngelList. Many angel investors in the early stages of your business are made up of your friends, family members, or advisers that know you, believe in you and your business, and want to help you get there.

- **Venture capital.** VC firms invest in high-growth businesses that have the potential for significant returns. You will need a solid business plan, a connection to a partner at the VC firm, former experience at a high-profile successful start-up, previous start-up success, or a direct line in or referral to pitch to attract venture capital. Most VCs won't meet with a start-up founder without these links. It is helpful to have a product demo or MVP to pitch, even for early stage funds. Remember, only 12,000 out of five million businesses that start every year ever get funded by a VC. That does not mean you won't be successful. AI has the chance to help democratize VC and help you succeed with much less capital.

- **Venture funds.** Meanwhile, venture funds continue to get bigger and bigger, and their average check size has increased. With start-ups, however, the true need for capital has decreased thanks to AI, and this has created a true market dislocation. The VC industry must, and will, change to keep pace with the plethora of new companies and great entrepreneurs that will emerge, who may need less capital now but will need more help, service, and mentorship to succeed.

- **Alternative lending.** There are alternative lending options such as online lenders or microfinance institutions that provide loans to small businesses. These are good solutions for retail or online commerce-enabled businesses that are already producing revenue.

It's important to remember that raising capital takes time and effort. You will need to have a strong "why," a tight business plan and business model, a product demonstration or recommended users or clients, financial projections, and a powerful pitch to attract investors or lenders. It may also be helpful to work with a financial adviser or consultant to help you navigate the fundraising process.

Entrepreneurship is a journey based upon a huge desire and passion to succeed, no matter what. Above all, it's an execution game.

At EMG, we believe there are seventy-three steps of execution you will need to take before you can exit your business successfully. These seventy-three steps can take many years. Completing them requires an entrepreneur to have a true mission and the will and passion to make it happen.

New product development

When Steve Jobs had the idea for the iPhone, legend has it that he was told by one of his advisers or someone on his team to conduct a focus group and discuss and show a sketch of the product he was thinking about launching. Jobs said, "People don't know what they want until you show it to them. That's why I never rely on market research."[27]

His point was a good one. True market and product innovation involves going to where the market is going, and sometimes true innovation can't be told and must be seen. Steve Jobs was a once or twice in a generation entrepreneur whose genius was in product innovation. Your genius may be in your ability to

---

[27] J Aten, "This is Steve Jobs's most controversial legacy. It is also his most brilliant," *Inc.* (19 January 2021), www.inc.com/jason-aten/this-was-steve-jobs-most-controversial-legacy-it-was-also-his-most-brilliant.html, accessed 8 July 2025

problem solve, care for customers, sell into an existing market, recruit great people, or market better than anyone in your industry. Whatever it is, leverage that strength and look to product innovation as another variable to build enterprise value through innovation.

New product development can be a key driver of growth for your company. Here are some best practices for new product development:

1. **Start with customer needs.** The best new products are those that solve a customer problem or address a need. Begin by understanding your customers' pain points, wants, and needs, and then develop a product that meets those needs. What can your product do better, faster, or more cheaply than others?

2. **Conduct market research.** Before investing resources into new product development, conduct market research to assess the viability of your idea. This can include surveys, focus groups, and analyzing market trends. It is important to have data and knowledge of where the market is today and where it is going, to add creditability to what you are building or launching.

3. **Create a cross-functional team.** New product development requires input from multiple departments, including research and development, marketing, and sales. It is key to

build a cross-functional team with members who have the skills and expertise necessary to develop and launch a successful product. Get your head of sales, marketing leader, or customer success lead in the room with you and your lead engineers or product specialists.

4. **Develop a prototype.** Once you have an idea and have conducted market research, create a prototype of the product. This will help you test the product and gather feedback from potential customers. Often called a minimal viable product (MVP), having an early prototype can excite investors, entice prospects, and help existing customers stay on board. When people see what is coming, they believe they are betting on a winner.

5. **Test and refine.** Test the product with potential customers and gather feedback. Use this feedback to refine the product and make improvements before launching.

6. **Develop a marketing plan or playbook.** Develop a marketing plan for the new product, including target audience, messaging, and channels for promotion. How will this product or service launch? What will the avenues be to getting traffic and brand or product awareness?

7. **Launch and track results.** Launch the product and track its performance. Monitor sales, customer feedback, and any other metrics that will help you evaluate the success of the product.

Remember that new product development can be a time-consuming and resource-intensive process, but the rewards can be significant and game-changing for your business. By following these best practices, you can increase your chances of developing a successful new product that drives growth for your small business.

Press release templates

Pre-social media, the way companies would announce new products, client or partner wins, or milestones would be via a press release and putting it on the wire. While still an important part of the marketing mix for any business, PR has changed. Public relations and press releases are important tools for businesses to communicate their message to the public and media but should be leveraged intensely by social and influencer media. It's no longer practical to think that once the release is dropped, people will hear about it.

A basic press release template should include:

- Your company logo
- Headline
- Sub-headline
- City, state, date
- Lead paragraph

- Quote
- Additional details
- Call to action
- Company information or boilerplate with URL and contact details

Here are some tips for creating effective press releases:

- **Write a compelling headline.** Your headline should grab the readers' attention and entice them to read the rest of the press release.

- **Have a strong lead.** Your lead should provide a summary of the key points in the press release and make the reader want to read more.

- **Use quotes.** Including quotes from key stakeholders or experts can add credibility and depth to your press release.

- **Provide details.** Include relevant details about your business, product, or service, and any supporting information or data.

- **Include a call to action.** Your press release should include a call to action, such as directing readers to your website or inviting them to attend an event.

Public relations

For public relations, here are some tips for getting started:

- **Identify your target audience.** Determine who you want to reach with your PR efforts: potential customers, industry influencers, or investors. Put yourself in the mind and through the eyes of your desired reader. Write down what it is that you would like them to take away from reading the press release.

- **Develop a messaging strategy.** Determine what message you want to communicate and how you want to position your business.

- **Build relationships with media.** Identify relevant journalists or media outlets and start building relationships with them by providing helpful information and insights. I have found personal handwritten notes or emails to be useful, which take the time to explain what you are doing, why you are doing it, and why that release is important, not just to you and your business but to the market.

- **Leverage social media.** Use social media to amplify your message and engage with your audience. Leverage and repost your releases or news. Comment, comment, comment. Get reshares from your ecosystem.

- **Monitor your coverage.** Keep track of your media coverage and use analytics to measure the impact of your PR efforts. Respond and create a dialogue with postings or comments from you, your team members, advisers, and board members. Create a swell of comments or activity with every release and posting.

Protecting your invention: Registering IP

In the Age of AI, the creation of ideas into businesses will accelerate at a pace we have never seen before. It seems that AI will become not just a factory of knowledge to be leveraged but a factory for ideas. In the right hands of the right founders—who are giving the right prompts, asking it the right questions, and connecting the dots on markets, people, and resources—its impact will be seismic. Now it is even more important for entrepreneurs to protect their IP to ensure it can't be stolen by competitors or copied by other entrepreneurs and AI models. Just as code is now, ideas will soon be generated by machines.

The best way for an inventor or entrepreneur to protect their IP is to seek government protection for their idea through patent law. Patents are the strongest way entrepreneurs can protect their invention and ensure others don't copy their product or service. Historically, the time needed to file and receive a patent can take up to three years, but the average patent is granted in eighteen months. The cost for filing a patent on average is over US$20,000, and the process is often complex, time-consuming, and expensive. Due to these reasons, the patent protection process has been historically only something that well-connected entrepreneurs or larger companies have pursued.

AI isn't just accelerating the need for patent protection; it's also helping to create a more cost-efficient and effective way for entrepreneurs to get patent protection. There is now a company, powered by AI, which helps inventors protect their IP. MyEdison.AI was created to help democratize the process for filing and receiving a patent and aids in accelerating the patent-filing process. MyEdison.AI helps entrepreneurs and inventors find out if patents have already been issued for similar products to theirs and then helps to design a patent filing that is unique to them.

MyEdison.AI also gives a potential valuation on the invention or IP as well as a prediction of the likelihood of the success of the filing process. Once filed, MyEdison.AI then provides a digital way to store, track, and maintain the IP. The result is a world where entrepreneurs are not hindered by the process or costs involved in protecting their IP. MyEdison.AI is a great example of how AI can be used to help entrepreneurs do more with less to help usher in this new entrepreneur revolution. In the next few years, the need for patent protection will explode and will be fueled by

AI's expansion, but even now entrepreneurs can help harness it to protect themselves and their businesses.

If you prefer not to use a service like MyEdison.AI, you can register your IP in the traditional way by following these steps with your IP counsel or attorney:

1. **Conduct a trademark search.** Before registering a trademark, conduct a search to make sure that the proposed mark is not already registered or being used by someone else in the same, or a similar, industry.

2. **File a trademark application.** Once you have determined that your proposed mark is available, file a trademark application with the USPTO. The application can be filed online or by mail.

3. **Register a domain name.** To do this, you can use a domain name registrar such as GoDaddy™, Namecheap, or Google Domains. Check to see if the desired domain name is available and then purchase it.

4. **Register social media profiles.** Create accounts on popular social media platforms such as Facebook, X, Instagram, and LinkedIn. Use your business name as the username.

It's important to note that registering IP can be a complex process, so it may be beneficial to seek the advice of an attorney who specializes in IP law.

Scoreboarding

Dashboarding is how for the last thirty years CXOs, entrepreneurs, and executives consumed mission-critical information or metrics from their software applications from the IT department. Today, software is the new fabric of every business in the world. Dashboards are common features for cloud-based applications as most have a layer to show the most important data from their applications. There is still the need for application and data agnostic information and insight.

We believe at EMG that with the rise of AI and available APIs, those protocols that help connect software applications and the data and information will make this even easier and more efficient. Today, these new capabilities make data liquid. With the rise of AI, that insight can now become more actionable than ever. The concept of "dashboards" within the enterprise are going to give way to scoreboards or "scoreboarding" for entrepreneurs and businesses of all sizes.

A scoreboard will provide data insights around your most important metrics, which can then be judged against your goals or peer group to measure your performance, not in a silo but with context.

The buzzwords that management consultants like McKinsey or Bain & Company put in the mainstream of business for this type of peer group or competitive group analysis per metric were "key performance indicators" (KPIs). KPIs were something that only the biggest companies could have at their fingertips due to harder-to-find and proprietary datasets. Today, AI makes those datasets easier to obtain per industry, per market, or per company size, so that every business—regardless of size—can now have KPIs specific to them.

An example of a useful KPI in your new company scoreboard would be "revenue per employee" (RPE). RPE would be measured by your business by taking your total revenue for the year and dividing that number by the number of employees you have. That discrete number is an interesting measure of your progress year to year—the idea being the higher that number the better—but in a vacuum (without context to your peers or to the market) it has less meaning.

Today, thanks to AI and scoreboard systems, any company can monitor their own KPIs via their own scoreboard to truly measure the execution and performance of their business in real time. Every business should have no fewer than ten and no more than twenty metrics or KPIs to measure on their scoreboard. Your company scoreboard can be viewed, monitored, measured, and shared in real time to you, your team, or your investors and stakeholders. Scoreboards are here to stay and are the future of performance, execution, and business management.

SCOREBOARDING YOUR BUSINESS

At EMG we have created a framework for you to begin to lay out and measure your most important metrics before getting your own business scoreboard at EMG.AI.

Business scoreboard KPIs tick sheet

KPI	Current score	Company goals	Competitors
Revenue	$45,230.00	$39,000 [+7.3%]	$25,000 [+20%]
Profit margin	32.0%	30% [+3%]	28% [+4%]
Users	206	175 [+16%]	110 [+20%]
Contracts	5	5	3 [+40%]
Revenue/ employee	$11,300	$7,000 [+21%]	$4,000 [+35%]
Job completion rate	85%	100% [−15%]	80% [+20%]
Retention rate	80%	100% [−20%]	70% [+10%]
Leads	250	200 [+25%]	90 [+105%]

SIX
Planning Your Successful Exit

As my friend Daniel Priestley says: "You will exit your business." You will either sell it commercially, transfer its ownership to your family, sell it to your employees with an employee stock ownership plan (ESOP), shut it down (God forbid), or die with it. The essential knowledge you need for that day when it comes—and it *will* come—is knowing what your business is worth. This question is now more important than ever, and it is something that you can ascertain in real time. It is also something that you should monitor, manage, and grow.

What's your business worth?

Your goal should be to exit your business at the top. With the market comparables, that is the price multiple paid when revenue or earnings are at the top of the market. This is why we have gone through the seventy-three components of the Entrepreneur's Roadmap in such painstaking detail and why we created EMG. We want you to maximize your value with your business, so you win. Win for you, for your family, for your team, for your investors and shareholders, and for all your stakeholders. Enterprise value—what your company is worth to a buyer—is tangible but also intangible. The intangibles are made up of what you could do for your buyer, how you could help them grow their businesses, and how you can grow their mind and market share.

What your business is worth is a number or value, but it is made up of so much more than that. Our goal is to help you maximize your value and show this to your customers, team members, and investors, and one day your shareholders.

My last software company was created with the mission and purpose of helping every business owner in the world discover their value for free or in a fraction of the time and cost usually needed to do it. It was born, as discussed earlier, from my work with the legendary Pete Musser who would ask every entrepreneur he met, "What do you think your business is worth?"

The story of BizEquity

BizEquity was created with a simple and powerful mission: to democratize business valuation knowledge for every business owner. Thanks to cloud computing environments and data as a service, or big data analysis, we were able to create the largest and most successful online way to value any business. BizEquity was born based upon the ability to provide to the business market what the real estate market has done for the last forty years; that is, to put a value on the underlying assets they are measuring.

Too often, as the IBIS World Research analysis shows, too few businesses valued themselves. IBIS Research determined that less than 2% of businesses every year valued themselves due to the costs, time, and complexity in valuing a business.[28]

We cracked the code on that by creating an online service that could help any business, pretty much anywhere, to value themselves. A business would and could simply go online at www.bizequity.com and begin their journey by entering information into our patented seven-step process.

This seven-step process of BizEquity allows any user to enter the following information online:

---

28 B McErlaine, "Business valuation firms in the US," IBISWorld (December 2024), www.ibisworld.com/united-states/industry/business-valuation-firms/4797, accessed 28 October 2025

- Industry
- Organizational type
- Location
- Revenue
- Costs
- IP
- Growth
- Recurring revenue
- Earnings or EBITDA
- Assets
- Liabilities

Based on inputting these figures, a valuation appears. You can continue to add more financial, performance, and operational detail to ensure a more and more accurate business valuation.

BizEquity started with a simple mission and has now been used by nearly a million business owners and CEOs to gain an understanding of their value. We had many trials and tribulations along the way. Miles Frost, my good friend and lead investor in our Series A round, passed away tragically. We made a pivot or change of direction with our business three years into it to sell the product via the channel to financial institutions as they could still uphold the mission of democratizing this knowledge while underwriting our ability to make the product better and grow. I successfully sold the business in 2019 to a wonderful investment and holding company, which had the leading media business-to-business owners and financial institutions in the United States. I stayed on well beyond my due (or earn-out) date to help protect the mission but also to ensure I didn't let the buyer down, who I had grown to respect immensely.

All in all, BizEquity was an incredible mission made up of incredible people I met through the journey, with lasting impact for all involved.

Wealth and retirement planning

I don't like the term "retirement planning." If you love what you do as an entrepreneur and leader, you will never retire, so let's call it "wealth planning." Too often, wealth managers look to market to entrepreneurs after they sell their business, when everyone wants to be their friend. Instead, good wealth managers and planners should look to find entrepreneurs before they sell and when they need their help the most. A good wealth manager—and one an entrepreneur wants to work with—should help them on their journey by introducing them to their resources to better manage the wealth they have now, and to grow their fortunes with their business. If a wealth manager invested in the promise of an entrepreneur before they sold their business, they would have that entrepreneur for life.

If you are like me, you truly believe you will be successful with your business if you have enough time to fulfill its mission. You are willing to bet on yourself with your business (or you wouldn't be reading this book), but you want to make sure your family will be OK if you run out of time.

Wealth planning should start before you have millions and when your dreams are bigger than your bank account. If you do proper wealth planning, you don't need retirement planning. That is the idea that you should have while you are investing in yourself to protect you or your family by finding a wealth adviser that cares about what you are doing and by taking steps to protect your financial livelihood.

These three things will help you on your journey by giving you the peace of mind that you have some sort of protection to go chase your dreams:

1. **Invest in an index fund monthly.** Sign up for Vanguard, Fidelity, or Robinhood, and do a monthly draw to a conservative index fund.

2. **Invest in insurance.** Get life insurance to protect your family while you build your business. It will give you reassurance, and when you're young it's cheap. I did that the first year of BizEquity, while I was newly married, to help me

better manage my risks and feel good for the risk I was taking. I am glad I did. It was cheaper back then as I was younger.

3. **Get a 401(k) for your company.** Once on payroll from the likes of ADP or Paychex you can get a 401 plan cost-effectively put in.

When it comes to more traditional retirement planning for you or the rest of your team, here are some additional insights:

- **Assess your current retirement savings.** Take stock of your current retirement savings and determine how much you will need for a comfortable retirement.

- **Define your retirement goals.** Determine how much money you need to save to meet your retirement goals. Consider factors like the lifestyle you want in retirement, your health, and how long you plan to work.

- **Create a retirement plan.** Once you know your retirement goals, work with a financial planner to create a retirement plan that fits your needs. This plan should include strategies for saving and investing, as well as ways to reduce taxes.

- **Maximize your retirement savings options.** As a business owner, you have several options for saving for retirement, such as a 401(k), IRA, SEP-IRA, or Simple IRA. These are government authorized and regulated retirement accounts in the US whereby the investor receives deferred tax treatment. Evaluate the pros and cons of each option to determine which one is best for you.

- **Stay on track.** Regularly review your retirement plan to ensure you are on track to meet your goals. Adjust as needed to keep your plan up to date.

- **Consider succession planning.** If you plan to retire and pass on your business to someone else, consider a succession plan. This plan should outline how your business will be transferred and who will take over after you retire.

- **Work with professionals.** Retirement planning can be complicated, so consider working with a financial planner, accountant, or attorney to help you make the best decisions for your business and retirement.

Exit planning

According to a CNBC study, 78% of entrepreneurs plan to fund their retirement from the sale of their business.[29] If 98% of companies or entrepreneurs have

---

29 L Ioannou, "Small biz owners ignoring succession advice: Poll," *CNBC* (13 April 2015), www.cnbc.com/2015/04/13/ew-small-biz-have-an-exit-plan.html, accessed 9 July 2025

not done a business valuation in the current year,[30] they are already leaving money on the table because they have not maximized what could be. That is why planning for your eventual exit is so important. Exit planning involves creating a strategy for the eventual sale or transfer of a business.

Here are some steps to take to carry out exit planning for your business:

1. **Define your goals and objectives.** Identify what you want to achieve through the exit process, such as maximizing the value of your business or ensuring a smooth transition for employees.

2. **Evaluate your business.** Conduct a thorough evaluation of your business, including financial performance, market position, and operational efficiency. This will help you determine the potential value of your business and identify any areas that need improvement.

3. **Develop a transition plan.** Create a detailed plan for how you will transfer ownership or control of the business. This may involve finding a buyer, grooming a successor, or transitioning to a family member.

4. **Consider tax implications.** Consult with a tax professional to understand the tax implications

---

30 Mercer Capital, "Only 2% of small businesses know this key fact" (18 July 2022), https://mercercapital.com/only-2-of-small-businesses-know-this-key-fact, accessed 9 July 2025

of selling your business and develop a plan to minimize taxes.

5. **Review legal agreements.** Review and update legal agreements such as buy–sell and operating agreements to ensure they align with your exit plan.

6. **Communicate with key stakeholders.** Communicate your exit plan with key stakeholders such as employees, customers, and suppliers. This will help minimize disruption and ensure a smooth transition.

7. **Monitor progress.** Continually monitor the progress of your exit plan and adjust it as needed to ensure that you achieve your goals.

8. **Conduct a financial sensitivity analysis.** A financial sensitivity analysis for a business is an examination of how changes in certain variables can impact a company's financial performance.

Conducting a financial sensitivity analysis

When you develop your financial plans and pro forma for future financial performance, you should create various scenarios around the most likely outcomes.

Often that means creating a high, medium, and low analysis based upon certain things that could occur, good and bad. This analysis is used to identify the degree of sensitivity of a company's financial results to changes in variables such as sales, costs, interest rates, exchange rates, or other key drivers. By performing a financial sensitivity analysis, a company can assess its potential vulnerabilities and develop a contingency plan to mitigate any negative impacts on its financial performance. This analysis can also help businesses to make more informed decisions about pricing, investments, and risk management.

To conduct a financial sensitivity analysis for your business, follow these steps:

1. **Define the financial variables.** Identify the key financial variables that impact your business, such as sales, expenses, interest rates, and taxes.

2. **Determine the range of values.** Estimate the possible range of values for each variable. For example, if your sales are affected by changes in the economy, you might estimate a range of 10 to 20% growth or decline.

3. **Create a financial model.** Use a spreadsheet or financial modeling software to create a model of your business's financials. Input your revenue and expense data, along with the values for each variable you identified in step 1.

4. **Test the model.** Run the model using the different values for each variable to see how they impact your financials. For example, if you input a 10% decline in sales, see how it impacts your profit and cash flow.

5. **Analyze the results.** Look at the results of the sensitivity analysis to determine which variables have the most significant impact on your business's financials. Use this information to make decisions about managing risk and taking action to mitigate potential negative impacts.

6. **Monitor the variables.** Continuously monitor the variables identified in your sensitivity analysis to stay informed about changes that may impact on your business's financial performance.

Selling your business

For an entrepreneur, selling a business can be a complex and time-consuming process. The best time to sell is often when you feel that growth could be accelerated by the acquirer and when you believe you have maximized your growth rate.

Here are some steps you can take to get started:

1. **Determine the value of your business.** Before selling your business, you need to determine its value. BizEquity.com is a great way to start.

2. **Prepare your business for sale.** Get your business in top shape for a sale by identifying and addressing any potential issues. This could include cleaning up your financials, updating your business plan, and improving your operations.

3. **Develop a marketing plan.** Create a marketing plan to promote your business to potential buyers. This could include listing your business for sale on business-for-sale websites, using social media to reach out to potential buyers, and working with an investment bank or M&A adviser to find the right buyer.

4. **Identify potential buyers.** Reference your work with the exit mapping process discussed later in the chapter.

5. **Negotiate the deal.** Once you have identified a potential buyer, you need to negotiate the deal. This includes agreeing on the terms of the sale, the purchase price and earn-outs, and staff hires or retainers.

6. **Close the deal.** After the terms of the sale have been agreed upon, you need to close the deal. This involves drafting and signing a purchase agreement, transferring ownership, and ensuring that all legal requirements are met. Please make sure you work with a proper business or corporate attorney or an M&A adviser, who can guide you through the entire process and help you get the best deal possible.

When do you sell your business?

Deciding on the best time to sell your business can be a complex and personal decision that depends on various factors, including:

- **Personal circumstances.** Your age, health, family dynamics, and financial situation may impact your decision to sell.

- **Market conditions.** The state of the economy and industry trends can influence the value of your business. The market comparables of selling prices are usually determined by sales, sales growth, and profitability.

- **Opportunities.** If you have an opportunity to sell your business to an eager buyer or strategic partner your time to sell may have arrived.

- **Goals and aspirations.** If you have achieved your goals and want to move on to new opportunities, selling your business may be the right decision.

Ultimately, when you should sell your business is you and your board's decision. Running a proper process with a good attorney and the right M&A advisory firm or investment can create a competitive process that will help to drive up the price of your business and ensure that it gets done.

Build your data room

It's never too early to document everything you have. A data room is an online storage folder of everything your business has done and what it plans to do. In a sense it represents your archives and the blueprint for your business's future.

Whether you are at day one or day 4,001 of your company's existence, you should build your data room now with your end in mind. Imagine what your data room or data store will have in it in five years' time. Imagine who will be going through it. What would you like to have populated in it? Categorize it now.

Task your team with constant execution and focus with the idea that whatever they do or contribute will one day be published in the data room. The contracts file, the press and marketing materials and mentions, the sales pipeline, and forecast creations. This process will impart discipline and value for your business.

Data rooms are now cost-effective and there are many interfaces to the software applications you currently use. This makes the ingest or intake of the materials much less time-consuming. The best companies begin with the end in mind. Your end goal should always be to build a masterpiece, whether you are one person in a garage or a team of 1,000 in the city.

Exit mapping

Exit mapping is the process of developing a strategy for how to exit or sell a business in the future. It involves identifying the goals and objectives for the exit, determining the optimal time to exit, and preparing the business for a successful sale.

Exit mapping is the proactive planning of the potential sale of your business to acquirers; an exercise that allows you to put down the universe of potential desired acquirers across a variety of rationale or reasons. For example, you could have built a new AI company in the CRM market that Salesforce may desire, a company that might not have a CRM solution yet, or a cloud-hosting provider looking to get into the application layer.

Here are some steps to consider when creating an exit map for your business:

1. **Define your goals.** Identify your personal and business objectives for the exit. This might include financial goals, retirement planning, or passing the business on to family members.

2. **Determine the best time to sell.** Research the market conditions and the broader market characteristics and industry trends to determine the best time to sell your business.

3. **Identify potential buyers.** Consider who might be interested in buying your business, such as competitors, investors, or employees. Make the list exhaustive. You may be surprised by who is interested in your business. If you list only ten or

twenty potential acquirers, you are not thinking big enough.

4. **Prepare the business for sale.** Conduct a thorough assessment to identify any areas that need improvement before putting the business on the market. Create the materials that you think would wow potential acquirers in terms of what you have built, why it is unique, and why they should care.

5. **Determine the value of the business.** Conduct a living valuation to determine the fair market value of the business. Include the value creation you may offer them in terms of what your product or service could do for their installed base of users or clients. Think bigger.

6. **Develop a marketing strategy.** Create a marketing plan that includes identifying potential buyers, creating marketing materials, and developing a sales strategy.

7. **Negotiate the sale.** Work with your advisers to negotiate the terms of sale, including the purchase price, payment terms, and other details.

8. **Execute the sale.** Once the terms have been agreed upon, work with your advisers to complete the sale and transfer ownership of the business. Often, having an investment bank, world-class law firm, or M&A adviser will help you get 5–10% more than you dreamed for your

business. Don't worry about the costs associated with the successful sale; they would only be costs assuming a successful outcome, if structured properly.

EXERCISE: Exit mapping

Create a list of all your potential acquirers (at least twenty) and order them by market segment and rationale for acquisition. List the clients and go-to-market partners. In each column, mark and rank the fit of your company. Analyze their pricing model and use cases for their products. Include any stated market intentions for their growth strategies, then map them to your business.

Exit your business successfully

Always prepare for the potential of selling your business. Everything you do to grow your business's value should be documented and viewed under the lens of: "What would an acquirer think if we did this?"

Preparing for an exit for your business requires careful planning and a focus on execution in every aspect that highlights your distinctive competencies (what makes your business, product, or service unique). Here are some tips to help you prepare:

- **Document your systems and processes.** Before you can sell your business, you need to have a clear understanding of your systems and processes. This includes everything from your financial statements to your operational procedures. Documenting these processes will make it easier for potential buyers to evaluate your business and understand how it operates.

- **Get your financials in order.** You need to have accurate and up-to-date financial statements to provide to potential buyers. This includes your balance sheet, income statement, and cash flow statement. Sometimes buyers want to ensure you have had an audit; that is, audited financials to validate your financial statements from a third-party accounting firm. This can cost US$5,000 a year, but it is well worth it to have at least two years before you sell. You may also need to provide projections for future performance. This is called a pro forma, or future financial projections. This can exist in separate spreadsheets but is also often contained in your board of directors' presentations, which will be in the data room.

- **Hire a management or growth consultant, or a coach.** Professional athletes have had coaches before they have thrown a ball; why not a professional entrepreneur? What used to be called a management consultant is now called a coach. A coach can help you identify areas where you can improve your business operations, which can increase the value of your business. They can also help you prepare for due diligence and work with potential buyers.

- **Create a deal room.** A deal room is a secure online space where you can share documents and information with potential buyers. This can include financial statements, legal documents, and other information that potential buyers may need to evaluate your business.

- **Choose an investment banker or M&A adviser.** M&A advisers can provide guidance and support throughout the exit process, from preparing your business for sale to negotiating the deal. You can find M&A advisers through your network, advisers board, peer group of fellow entrepreneurs, accountant, industry associations, business networks, or online directories. It's important to choose an M&A adviser who has experience working with businesses similar to yours and a track record of successfully completing deals. They can provide valuable advice on everything from valuation to deal structuring and can help you navigate the complexities of the exit process. Often, what may seem expensive (3% of the exit value) will pale in comparison to the increase that they can get you for your business.

What does a successful exit look like?

When I was looking to raise capital for my last company, I didn't necessarily foresee selling the company, but I wanted to ensure I had proper representation. With the help of a member of my advisory board, I sourced a potential world-class publicly listed company who might have been interested to invest. I provided a list of "friends of the company" that may be investors, but I also still hired the investment bank.

When you work with an investment bank, you pay for the process they run and the surety they provide to a buyer or investor. In my case, the potential investment company produced a term sheet for an investment with the option to acquire the company. This term sheet opened up the board members' minds as well as my own as to the potential to sell the company. As they say, you never know how attractive you are until you have one suitor.

This one term sheet ended up opening up a competitive process once other investors and acquirers realized that we were in the market via our investment banker. My second offer came in and it was for the full purchase of my company at a fair price. If I had not run the process with a proper investment banker and investment bank, I would never have had the option to sell the business at that time.

SEVEN
The New Age Of Entrepreneurship

We are in the Age of AI, which will change the shape and course of global entrepreneurship. AI is the fifth revolution in business since the dawn of trade, and it will reshape society and business life. AI makes knowledge liquid, it manufacturers knowledge work and knowledge workers, it will make networks of connection seamless, and it will impact every aspect of society and change the way we work forever. It makes the cost of creation fall to nearly zero. Cloud computing in 2015 helped to decrease the costs of starting software companies by 50%; now AI will decrease the cost of starting all businesses by 50%.

According to IDC, the global total spend on AI "will contribute US$19.9 trillion to the global economy through 2030" and "every new dollar spent on business-related AI solutions will contribute US$4.60 into the global economy."[31] There has never been such an investment in terms of actual dollars into a technology or market sector in the history of the world. Why? Because every modern company is in part a software or technology company. Today, AI represents to modern businesses what oil and gas was to the automobile sector but for the entire economy. It's such an exciting place to be.

The democratization of AI

AI will not just democratize engineering and enable anyone to become a coder or an engineer but it will also democratize entrepreneurship, making ideas ubiquitous. Entrepreneurship will now avail itself to everyone because of the wide-ranging consequences of having knowledge of everything on tap.

Today there are roughly 594 million entrepreneurs.[32] By 2040, AI will help create over one billion entrepreneurs.[33] AI democratizes knowledge of every func-

---

31 IDC Research, "IDC: Artificial intelligence will contribute $19.9 trillion to the global economy through 2030 and drive 3.5% of global GDP in 2030" (17 September 2024), https://my.idc.com/getdoc.jsp?containerId=prUS52600524, accessed 9 July 2025
32 M Kiniulis, "Entrepreneur Statistics: Industry insights," MarkinBlog (19 October 2023), www.markinblog.com/entrepreneur-statistics, accessed 18 August 2025
33 AI TechPark, "Empowering one billion entrepreneurs by 2040: The AI and blockchain revolution" (10 July 2023), https://ai-techpark.com/the-ai-and-blockchain-revolution-for-entrepreneurs, accessed 18 August 2025

tional area of a business and supports the creation, growth, operations, and exit functions. The difference will be an entrepreneur's ability to execute on their journey and the proprietary IP they own or that is protected.

Every person from anywhere in the world will have the ability to become an entrepreneur, and businesses will be created in seconds through AI. In the future, it won't matter about a person's background, education, experience, or network; everyone is equal in the eyes of AI. Social media has democratized communication through networks of connectivity and with wi-fi access like Starlink. It's now the case that anyone with a phone, a tablet, a computer, glasses, or headsets, or simply using their voice, will be able to access a living library of knowledge. AI-enabled digital agents will soon give way to autonomous agents that function as employees or team members to accomplish their essential business processes. It's a brave new world for sure.

AI democratizes entrepreneurship by democratizing creation

Today you can go into a Google search box and search for anything. You can open ChatGPT and can ask it anything. One day, you will be able to go to FoundersGPT or EMG.AI, simply type in the idea for the business you want to create and then generate an AI-powered "business in a box" that's situated in the cloud. Imagine speaking your idea into your AI computing device, phone, or computer and—whoosh—your business has been created. You will have armies of AI agents accomplishing your needed tasks, virtual SDRs prospecting and selling for you, and your product created seamlessly.

Billion-dollar companies will be created that only have five or ten employees. Businesses will become global in an instant. They will be streamed in a sense like song catalogs are streamed on Spotify. Creativity will accelerate because AI will make attributes and characteristics like intuition and empathy, which great entrepreneurs have in spades.

Warren Buffett, in one of his famous annual letters for Berkshire Hathaway, wrote about the industrial shifts that have occurred over time and how they have impacted the economy and created new jobs and industries after the agrarian society was transformed by the industrial revolution.[34] Before automobiles were invented, there would never have been the need for tires for cars, gasoline stations, auto shops and repair stores, car washes, valets, or even parking garages.

Every technological revolution has ushered in new economies and opportunities for entrepreneurs.

---

34 W Buffett, "Berkshire Hathaway Inc Shareholder Letter" (2024), www.berkshirehathaway.com/letters/2024ltr.pdf, accessed 27 October 2025

THE NEW AGE OF ENTREPRENEURSHIP

Since the dawn of the internet in the 1990s, new roles, companies, industries, and markets have emerged. Millions of e-commerce companies and online stores have been created. New fulfillment companies, technology services, hosting providers, and software companies have entered the market. Companies like Amazon and eBay have helped to create hundreds of thousands of entrepreneurs who have successfully leveraged their infrastructure to create their own businesses.

Mobile phone companies like Apple have created millions of entrepreneurs through their App Store. Companies like Uber could not have occurred before the mobile phone. The internet gave birth to new real estate markets, such as the one Airbnb created for millions of property owners. These new companies, jobs, and professions didn't exist before the last technology revolution.

Think about AI. What new companies, industries, markets, and jobs will be created because knowledge is now liquid and time can be manufactured? These new opportunities will reshape the economy of tomorrow for you, your children, and your grandchildren. Your descendants will have jobs or build companies in industries that didn't exist ten, twenty, or thirty years ago.

The opportunities are huge and there are no rules now about how entrepreneurs will need to be in the years ahead. Everything is on the table. Go to where the market is going and create your company in the future based upon how the world will change and the needs that will arrive for consumers and businesses. What companies can be built on top of the ChatGPT, OpenAI, or xAI ecosystems of knowledge?

The role of the developer as cocreator developers

One major new market space that will be created is software engineering. There are over 28,700,000 software engineers in the world today, according to Evans Research.[35] There are over 1.5 million firms or agencies globally. That number looks to increase threefold in the next ten years. This number is off by 100% in the next ten years.

Jensen Huang, the CEO of Nvidia, has said famously that "anyone can be a programmer with AI."[36] Imagine having your own personal engineer to create for you what you see and where you think the markets will be going. AI democratizes creation and the cocreation developer (CCD) will be the way entrepreneurs

---

35 Evans Data Corporation, "Worldwide professional developer population of 24 million projected to grow amid shifting geographical concentrations" (21 May 2019), https://evansdata.com/press/viewRelease.php?pressID=278, accessed 9 July 2025

36 PJ Pax, "5 AI tools that I used to make my first $1000 as a no-code developer," *Medium* (27 January 2025), https://beingpax.medium.com/5-ai-tools-that-i-used-to-make-my-first-1000-as-a-no-code-developer-06e3ae22e0d0, accessed 9 July 2025

around the world build new businesses and harness the power of AI.

More and more developers are becoming independent and leading larger consulting or development firms. EMG.AI believes there will be over 10 million independent software firms made up of fewer than five full-time equivalents (FTEs) or CCDs by 2030. Why? Because the role of the traditional software developer will change. Developers will become cocreators for businesses and consumers. Everyone and every business will have their own CCD, in the same way that people are talking about having their own digital agents. The CCD will be partly automated and partly FTE. It will be delivered by an entrepreneur. Much like the great VC investor believes every student will have their own personal automated tutor that understands how they learn and helps them learn better, businesses will have their own dedicated CCD to help them get out new products and services and perform functions that augment their staff.

The CCDs' talents won't just lie in their ability to write software code to build logic and make things work. Developers will be solution and creation architects who will build works of art through businesses. Software will become like oxygen that businesses function on. These new types of AI agencies or software cocreation engineers will form their own businesses because now they can do more with less. Every young smart engineer can now create their own LLCs or C Corporations for their businesses to benefit from small business ownership and being the entrepreneurs of their own lives.

Rather than thinking about how many engineering jobs will be lost, we should think about how many new people will form new businesses to take advantage of this trend because they are using AI to deliver software development projects that now take a fraction of the time or need a fraction of the engineers to deliver them. Now David will be able to take on the Goliaths like Accenture or Wipro in the battle for delivering AI solutions in the next five or ten years to businesses all around the world. Every business will have a digital agent just like they have websites, social media presences, or apps. Someone will have to deliver these and stand by the work of them.

The story of AI code insurance

With the proliferation of new AI software agencies, there will be a myriad of challenges and opportunities arising. For one, the software engineer forming his or her new business will need to know the seventy-three steps they need to execute to become a successful business. Additionally, companies will demand that their work must be assured or insured. Just like when construction companies and developers build homes or apartment complexes, it will be mandated that software companies will have to deliver "surety bonds" on their builds. Likewise, the companies of the future will demand some form of AI insurance on what they have paid for and ingested.

Today, Cyber insurance policies stop short of providing this layer of surety around risk. AI projects and solutions leverage third-party content and code that is often not licensed or shared. There is IP risk, contract risks with open-source licensing, and infrastructure risks with the underlying code and models that solutions will be built upon.

That is why EMG.AI has created and incubated the first-ever AI code insurance company of its kind, leveraging the first-ever AI-enabled code intelligence platform, The Code Registry. The Code Insurance company with CodeCover and its developer ensure product lines help these new CCDs get started in building their successful AI businesses. The company is led by Dan Brennan, a great software entrepreneur who helped to create the first software surety bonding business, Gladwyne Software Surety, with his founder at the time Mort Goldman. Dan will lead the effort at CodeCover.AI to help protect AI code for developers and businesses deploying it.

Democratizing the VC industry

AI will democratize the venture capitalist industry.

A very small number of businesses actually receive venture capital (VC) funding, with some estimates suggesting it is less than 0.05% of all start-ups or 1/12,000. While VC-backed start-ups may get significant media attention, the odds of a business securing this type of funding are extremely low, and founders must think how their business can stand out and look to alternative sources of capital. These alternative sources can come from government economic programs, angel investing, or new crowdfunding platforms.

There are only 41,000 VC firms globally, according to PitchBook.[37] Why should only 12,000 companies—based upon who they know, where they went to school, or where they live—get financed by early stage investment capital? The promise of AI is that the best companies, ideas, and entrepreneurs will be able to get funded, regardless of who they are or where they come from.

Great markets are created when there is a congruence of two or more trends that come together to form a great market or opportunity. For the democratization of VC, they are:

1. **AI.** The ability for knowledge, networks of people and capital, and resources to be liquid.

2. **Streaming and internet access.** The ability for anyone around the world to get online cheaply and quickly and consume video.

---

37 K Knickerbocker, "What is venture capital and how does it work?" *PitchBook* (3 September 2024), https://pitchbook.com/blog/what-is-venture-capital, accessed 9 July 2025

3. **Government policy.** The ability for crowdfunding and online investing into private businesses.

To help give more access to entrepreneurs looking to have their new companies and businesses receive start-up or growth investment capital, we believe at EMG.AI there has to be a better way. Think about how shows such as *Shark Tank* in the US or *Dragons' Den* in the UK have commercialized start-up investing and brought entrepreneurship into the mainstream. What if the judges on those shows were the four million viewers who are watching the entrepreneurs pitch? What if viewers could vote with their wallet via an app in real time? What if the ability for entrepreneurs to get their message out was democratized to everyone in the world so that anyone interested in their market, product, or service can access it?

Meet Founder Studio (FounderStudio.AI), which will be the first-ever live-streamed entrepreneurs' network where entrepreneurs from all over the world can pursue funding for their businesses in real time. We hope to democratize VC and help millions of entrepreneurs gain access to vital capital to fulfill their dreams. For viewers and investors, we hope to give access to pick entrepreneurs that can generate venture-like returns of their investments. Why should you just be able to bet on a game on an app? With Founder Studio, you can bet on entrepreneurs and their businesses and "Be your own VC."

Taxes: No longer a political issue

Taxes—the way governments around the world receive funding for their essential services through putting a levy or percentage tax on income, sales, profits, investment gains, business, and death—will need to change.

Voters and citizens will now demand transparency. Because of AI, this transparency will now be more readily available. Regardless of your political leanings or persuasion, it is something that every citizen and taxpayer should demand and every country around the world will instill and embed in the future. The auditing of government taxpayer dollars at such a mass scale is the first true use of AI in the history of government.

The founding fathers of the United States would be proud that citizens will now have a say not just in their vote but how their taxpayer dollars will be used to fund programs and fund government. This is the first step in a global movement that governments around the world will embrace to ensure that their taxpayer money will be used more efficiently by and for the people of the country.

Taxing the future

Entrepreneurs fix things. Entrepreneurs create products, services, and new markets. Entrepreneurs create jobs and revenue for their businesses that contribute to the federal government, both in terms of the actual taxes paid on sales and profits, and employee payrolls. When companies sell their shareholders pay again in the form of capital gains or taxes on the gains of the shares they own in the business, these capital gains taxes can reach as high as 30% when you factor in state taxes to the 20% mandatory floor.

Additionally, 49.3% of all taxes received by the government in the United States are collected from income taxes.[38] 70% of all those taxes are from employees from the private sector or business in the US. According to the US Treasury, 11% of all other taxes collected are collected from taxes on corporations and businesses. Social security taxes on employees from private sector jobs adds another 15%. In total, business or entrepreneur job creation contributes nearly 85% of all tax dollars.

The creation of entrepreneurs and policies that support business growth is essential for any government to survive and function. In fact, governments around the world should be today figuring out how they can create more entrepreneurs, not less, through incentivizing more people to create businesses as entrepreneurs.

In 1765, the British parliament—after winning the costly French and Indian War—passed a new tax called the Duties in American Colonies Act 1765. It was not

---

38 FiscalData, "How much revenue has the U.S. government collected this year?" (30 September 2024), https://fiscaldata.treasury.gov/americas-finance-guide/government-revenue, accessed 9 July 2025

meant to incite a riot or the reaction that it did, but it hit a chord with the colonial citizens as they felt it was unfair to be taxed for paying for something they did not vote for but that was done "for them" by the administrative parliamentary state. In that case it was the tax imposed for stationed British soldiers in the colonies; something their American brothers and sisters did not vote for. Unlike other taxes, this tax felt different to the colonists as it passed through to all the citizens, not just the merchant class. This tax would prove to be a galvanizing force, which helped to bring all the citizens together against those who sought to alter their liberty.

In the US, short-term capital gains, which are typically held by traders and employees and executives, is already taxed as ordinary income rates approaching 40% for the highest earners before state taxes are applied. The previous administration in the US proposed tax hikes looking to move up long-term capital gains, which are gains from founders of companies often and the investors behind these companies to the highest levels in 100 years (42.5% before state taxes). What if this new heightened tax on the entrepreneur class, who take the economic risk to hire teams of people and build companies that do things for people and business better, faster, and more cheaply, is implemented?

We are witnessing the second industrial revolution with the rise of AI, which will make "brain muscle" liquid to create new enterprises and automate logic and tasks, just as the first industrial revolution made "muscle power" available for mass manufacturing of goods.

The first industrial revolution created the consumer-led economy, which helped to proliferate democracies everywhere. The second industrial revolution will create mass entrepreneurialism to enable "mass creation" of companies, not just things. Yet, at the time when we should be incentivizing and subsidizing entrepreneurship and investment, we are instead looking to douse the flames of this fire by taxing its creation.

Taxes have become the sort of political discussion that polarizes people into the binary political world that exists. If you are for lower taxes, you may be labeled a right-wing Conservative. The truth is—and always has been—that lower taxes are good for all when directed at the producers of job growth, the creators and innovators. In the US, the entrepreneur or small business owner is responsible for most of the new job creation and growth in real wages for America's working class. Our greatest threat as a nation will not be from China, Russia, or an AI-enabled cyborg but from our unwillingness to help spur on entrepreneurship, which is the greatest export, by crippling them with taxes and burgeoning regulations.

Although two thirds of Americans feel they pay too much in federal income taxes,[39] it appears that an even smaller percent pays taxes today. The upshot is

---

39 AP NORC, "Majorities view local, state, and federal taxes as too high and delivering too little value for people like them" (28 January 2024), https://apnorc.org/projects/majorities-view-local-state-and-federal-taxes-as-too-high-and-delivering-too-little-value-for-people-like-them, accessed 9 July 2025

that more taxpayers are either not working or working for the government than workers in the private sector who are paying federal taxes. So many opportunities exist within the private sector if government limits involvement via taxation and regulation, with entrepreneurship offering the safest road to financial security for many Americans.

The entrepreneur or small business owner has been the engine of private sector job creation throughout the history of the US. As of 2024, the average business owner in the US runs a business that is estimated to be worth around US$1,232,451 according to the market leading business valuation service BizEquity. To climb into this club of successful businesses, the average business owner or entrepreneur mortgaged their future by taking out personally guaranteed small business loans, i.e., they are not funded by angels or VC or private equity firms. In fact, fewer than 12,000 companies every year are funded by VC or private equity firms. More than 99.7% of businesses are either self-funded or self-financed by a bank loan that is personally signed or guaranteed.

Imagine as an entrepreneur or business owner you are one of the lucky 10% that have successfully sold your business after years of investment, risk, grit, time, and self-determination. Your ultimate tax burden through that life cycle after years of hardships would be as follows:

1. Annual income tax rate: anywhere from 25 to 40%.

2. State taxes during that time: anywhere from 2 to 10%.

3. Property taxes on real estate and possibly equipment: +/–5%.

4. Sales taxes: 6–9%.

5. Payroll taxes to have the gift of paying for your employees: +6%.

6. If successful, capital gains will take 25–42.5%.

7. When you pass away, if not properly protected, expect another 40%.

A study cited at the ASU+GSV Summit for educational technology revealed that today 72% of high school students aspire to become an entrepreneur.[40] AI will democratize entrepreneurship, and enable everyone in the world to have the opportunity to become an entrepreneur. This is the miracle of AI.

According to the Global Entrepreneurship Monitor (Babson College), Americans are starting and running their own businesses at record levels in conjunction with a post-pandemic shift led by women and people of color.[41] Nearly one in five adults are in the process of founding a business or have done so in the past

---

40 M Moe and B Peus, "EIEIO… Here comes the sun," *Dash Media* (22 April 2024), www.dashmedia.co/p/eieiohere-comes-the-sun, accessed 9 July 2025

41 V Rodriguez, "GEM report: U.S. entrepreneurial activity returns to historic high," *Babson* (26 March 2025), http://entrepreneurship.babson.edu/gem-usa-2025, accessed 9 July 2025

three-and-a-half years. This means that businesses are introducing innovation, creating jobs, and contributing to the competitiveness of the US economy.

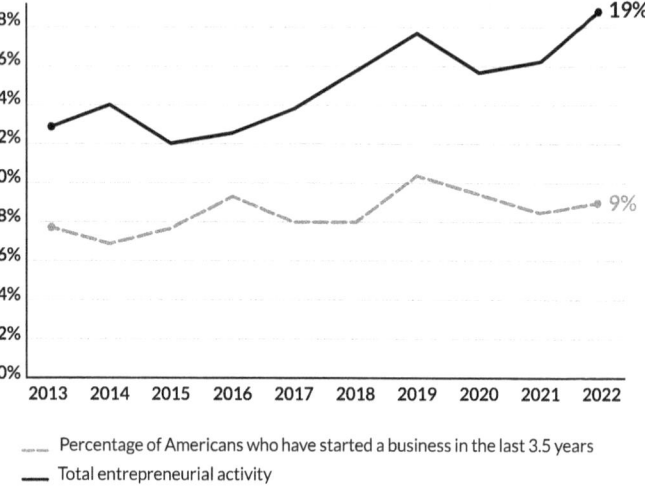

A record share of Americans have their own businesses

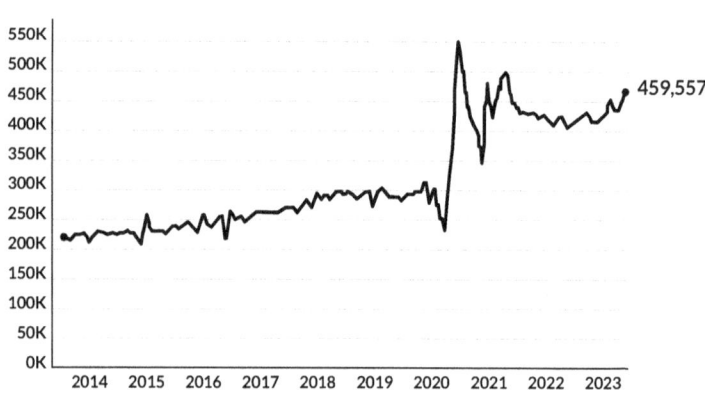

The US is adding nearly 500,000 new businesses a month (Source: US Census Bureau)

As these charts illustrate, and the data suggests, entrepreneurship is on the rise. Let's keep the momentum we have and not look for ways to hasten its accession. We should pull together as a nation and not be a country of "red and blue" states as President Obama so eloquently stated at the 2004 Democratic National Convention.[42]

Tax incentives to support growth and entrepreneurship should not be a "red and blue" issue. Supporting entrepreneurship is critical at this time when so many young people hold it in such high regard and the nation and the world needs its growth to propel its citizens to be able to pursue "Life, Liberty, and the pursuit of Happiness." It should not be a political football to simply divide a country and world that is already divided.

We are in the middle of a critical time when AI could help democratize entrepreneurship for everyone as knowledge and networks of relationships and capital are made more liquid. Supporting entrepreneurship through lower taxes not higher long-term capital gains rates should be on the table. As Lawrence Summers, the former treasury secretary of the United States, once said, "Washington is focused on the wrong things."

---

42 DA Frank and ML McPhail, "Barack Obama's address to the 2004 Democratic National Convention: Trauma, compromise, consilience, and the (im)possibility of racial reconciliation," *Rhetoric and Public Affairs*, 8/4 (Winter 2005), 571–593, www.jstor.org/stable/41940015, accessed 9 July 2025

We should focus on growth. Entrepreneurship is the critical vehicle, or weapon, to create it. Entrepreneurship is one of the things the United States does extremely well; it's time we focus on ways to democratize it through incentivizing its creation not penalizing it through higher long-term capital gains rates.

The point of the article I published at Real Clear Market entitled "The Stamp Act of 2025," during the summer of 2024 prior to the elections in the US, argued that economies will be built on the creation process of new businesses from entrepreneurs and how they will flourish, which will fuel their tax receipts. Vilifying entrepreneurs, who come in all political persuasions, races, and creeds, was not just unfair but not smart for government, business, and the global living standard. Taxes which used to be a political division based upon if you were a Republican or a Democrat, a Liberal or Conservative, will no longer be viewed through a political lens. Taxes will be revolutionized.

Taxes are a cost on creation

Governments will need to look beyond their simple lenses on increasing their tax rates to bring in more spend and balance their budgets. Governments' spend will be able to utilize AI technology and autonomous agents to ensure no graft or misuse. All tax dollars will be able to be audited daily.

Taxing entrepreneurs will be limiting to their growth. The countries with the lowest taxing on creation of businesses will be the ones that will win during the Age of AI. Taxes on entrepreneurs and the role of government need to change. Like the great economist Art Laffer illustrated through the Laffer curve made famous by Steve Forbes, increased tax revenue decreases at a certain point as taxes increase.

I argued in my book *The Mission Corporation* that governments around the world should create a new tax policy for entrepreneurs that will create businesses that create jobs, give back to their communities, and offer stock incentive programs to their employees. Governments should offer a special lower flat tax rate for businesses that are mission corporations to be created.

A mission corporation is one whereby the mission of the business is tangible and beneficial to the market they serve and that promotes a culture of meritocracy, giving, and learning. AI is the perfect market sector that can accelerate this. Domination and success for countries and governments will be based on their ability to create companies and entrepreneurs that innovate and embrace AI to deliver new capabilities that improve efficiency and effectiveness in the markets they serve.

AI will democratize entrepreneurship. Governments need to add to this ten-times force of acceleration and embrace the momentum that AI will bring to entrepreneurship, to fuel its growth to create more entrepreneurs through more and better tax incentives. The future of raising the living standard and individual freedom and liberty will be based on it. Everyone is an entrepreneur of their own lives, and everyone can become an entrepreneur.

It's time to right our policies and create the underlying infrastructure through networks and education to serve them and thus serve society.

Conclusion: What Does The Future Look Like For Entrepreneurs?

We are entering a renaissance of entrepreneurship that will change the world because of AI. The great new companies of tomorrow will be built by a band of three to five team members that share a common purpose and who are willing to focus on solving a specific problem. These new entrepreneurs will have the benefits of a trillion dollars of R&D at their fingertips with the help of new AI LLMs and AI sales and marketing tools that will help them penetrate global markets with a post, thanks to social media platforms like X, LinkedIn, YouTube, Facebook, and TikTok. Entrepreneurs around the world will remake economies globally as they add jobs, opportunities, and tax revenue to the countries they are domiciled in.

The old political arguments around taxation of businesses will no longer be bifurcated. Economies and countries around the world will learn that their most precious national resource is not just what is in the earth but who inhabits it: the entrepreneur. Entrepreneurs will become the rare commodity that countries will want to nurture with tax structures and incentives that will get introduced to keep or import them.

During the renaissance in the 1400s and 1500s, Italy paid to import artists because beauty and culture was how their countries would be judged. In the future, countries will be judged by the number of entrepreneurs they produce who are adding to the economy and society by creating wealth and meaning with the companies and communities of talent they are building.

Retooling won't be about manufacturing but around entrepreneurship, which will be the skill of tomorrow. Entrepreneurs will need to not just be born but be made. The artisans and artists of tomorrow will be the entrepreneur. Their palates and paints will be AI tools and technologies to remake the world and help you get stuff done more brilliantly and efficiently than ever before. Whether you are building a manufacturing business in Kolkata, India, like my friend Naman Shah, or an AI-based SaaS business, like Stephen Gray in London, UK, you will need to execute on a set of deliverables to have and build a solid and scalable business and will eventually have your own digital agent or mentor to help you grow your business.

CONCLUSION

The future of entrepreneurship will be AI enabled and driven by mission-led founders that can imagine things that machines just can't dream up yet. These new entrepreneurs can connect the dots on markets, relationships, and ideas that logic won't be able to discern. AI holds great societal risks with its ability to displace millions of workers fulfilling redundant tasks or functions. Entrepreneurship holds the key for how AI can be leveraged to change the world for the better, creating millions of new jobs and trillions of dollars of economic impact and new wealth creation for those with agency and conductive power to bring together the virtual orchestra.

The new entrepreneurs that will be born in the Age of AI will find holes and opportunities in the market, connect people and relationships to form businesses, and drive sales, while leveraging AI tools and agents to do more with less. These entrepreneurs will pull at the hearts and minds of customers through rich content marketing and stories that evoke feeling and can be created in an instant by AI agents.

These entrepreneurs will manage people by aligning them and their passions to the functions and tasks that need to be executed and outsourcing redundant tasks through an army of AI agents they subscribe to. The entrepreneurs of tomorrow will realize they will create the best teams by helping their non-digital (non-AI agent) team members they do have to prepare for their own hero's journey.

Entrepreneurs in the future will be more like the great entrepreneurs of the past, but there will be many millions more of them. They will have the hearts and missions of the entrepreneurs that were born after the industrial revolution but before the internet revolution of the 1990s and early 2000s. Those entrepreneurs were not solely driven by decision sciences and perfecting decision making and leveraging finance and capital markets, but based on ideals or ideas to revolutionize an industry. Many pre-AI entrepreneurs of the last twenty-five years were based on logic and non-emotional decision making via data they could correlate.

Now the magic of company creation will be in seeing what may not be logically correlated but can be dreamed of and felt by customers and the market, not by machines. Machine learning and AI-based logical decision making is now a service in the form of LLMs. Entrepreneurs will have the magic of innovation, invention, and agency in getting stuff done and bringing things together. Their special sauce will be in their humanity and creativity.

What is needed today and tomorrow will be driven and purpose-led individuals with big ideas and even bigger hearts that will see that the opportunity lies at the intersection of machines and humans. Big emotional quotients will be more important than large intellectual quotients. Harvard, Oxford, and Penn give way to Claremont, Drexel, Golden Gate,

CONCLUSION

Aberdeen, Glasgow, Newcastle, St. Joe's, and the University of Life.

AI is democratizing entrepreneurship, making it cheaper and easier to start and grow businesses at warp speed. Welcome to the age of big ideas and even bigger missions, where execution and agency will be paramount. Mercenaries and logical- and science-driven entrepreneurs are yesterday; that component will be in the machines, LLMs, and agents that will be leveraged by the entrepreneur. Today, what is needed is the heart and courage of a lion; the brains of Grok; ChatGPT or OpenAI; Claude or Gemini; and hopefully the roadmap and guidance of EMG.AI.

The world will see two billion entrepreneurs by 2040 and the first billionaire that has built his or her company with two or fewer employees. We want you to be one of them.

Key takeaways from this book

I wrote this book to help usher in and democratize entrepreneurship by putting this proven knowledge base—born from building and scaling multiple technology companies—into a format that all entrepreneurs can use: an Entrepreneur's Roadmap, at EMG.AI.

I would like you to take away the following from this book:

- Entrepreneurs are the stars of tomorrow and will change the world.
- AI will democratize entrepreneurship by making the creation process of business instant, leading to a renaissance of entrepreneurship.
- Intuition and emotional intelligence (EQ) will now be the entrepreneurial super-power.
- Since AI is making creating businesses so easy, you will need to protect your invention and build your IP today before someone else does. (Go to MyEdison.AI.)
- Entrepreneurship is a journey, and like a journey it starts with a purpose bigger than yourself in order for it succeed.
- Your business journey in the Age of AI will need a roadmap to ensure you get the essentials of creating and growing a business done.
- You can do it. You just need the support and a guide to your journey to know where you are going and how to get things done.
- Knowledge, connections, capital, and know-how are now liquid, but you need to know the right questions to ask and where to find them.

- EMG Worldwide, Inc., and our URL, EMG.AI, was created to help democratize entrepreneurship and provide the first-ever entrepreneurs' agent.

Join the movement as we build the most powerful community of entrepreneurs the world has ever known.

What's next?

Visit EMG.AI to join our global entrepreneur network and get your own entrepreneur's roadmap. We are offering free memberships for the first 1,000 members who are reading this book or referred to us online and sign up.

Our mission is to help democratize entrepreneurship. We are doing this by giving away our patent-pending and proven roadmap for entrepreneurs that has helped to build hundreds of successful businesses. This roadmap was amassed over twenty-five or more years of experience in helping entrepreneurs fulfill their missions and individual journeys.

Go to EMG.AI and join our movement to democratize entrepreneurship. We want to help you win.

Acknowledgments

I want to thank my wife Meredith, mother Louise, and kids Harrison and Catherine for always believing in me. Harrison and Catherine for always saying to me and others, "My daddy has written two books," and inspiring me to write more. I am so excited for my kids and the billion others around the world who will have the chance to pursue their dreams and purpose thanks to the transformational power of AI that will democratize entrepreneurship.

I also wish to thank my wonderful editor, Victoria Doxat, who helped me with *The Mission Corporation* in 2020, for being amazing and helping me bring this new one to life; always believing I had something important to say. I also wish to thank my friends and colleagues, Andrew Yeo and Ben Daugherty, who helped as my research assistants in putting this together. Thanks also to Daniel Priestley, who gave birth to the idea in the early days of BizEquity that I should be an author, and is a constant source of wisdom and friendship as we both build our families and companies in different continents and go through our entrepreneurship journeys together.

The Author

Michael Marsh Carter is a seven-time software entrepreneur and was the founder and CEO of BizEquity, the world's leading online business valuation software provider that helped to serve over 500,000 businesses around the world, now part of Advance Media. Mike was the youngest ever executive officer of publicly traded company Safeguard Scientifics, having helped to take US Interactive – one of the first Internet Professional Services – public, reaching over a US$1billion dollar valuation.

Mike is the holder of ten software patents across early artificial intelligence related to business intelligence, business valuation software, and cloud computing.

He is the author of two previous books, *What's Your Business Worth*, and *The Mission Corporation*. Mike is also the Co-Founder of The Mission Capitalist Club, a private members club and think tank for entrepreneurs. Mike has been called one of the top 100 people in Global Fintech by Hot Topics and is considered a leading US-based software entrepreneur and an active private venture investor.

With EMG.AI, Mike is creating the first agent for entrepreneurs and AI-centric venture operating company with a mission to help democratize and help over one million entrepreneurs.

Find out more at

🌐 EMG.AI